VIEWS
OF
LABOUR AND GOLD

A reprint of a book on political and moral economy

by

WILLIAM BARNES

FIDUCIA PRESS

2003

VIEWS
OF
LABOUR AND GOLD

by

WILLIAM BARNES

First published in 1859
by
JOHN RUSSELL SMITH
LONDON

Foreword by Fr Andrew Phillips
Introduction by Ken Griffiths

Book Design   Roy Gallop and Ken Griffiths
Photographic Processing   John Brewer
Typing Services   Leighanne Gough
Photographs   Carol Griffiths

Foreword © Fr Andrew Phillips 2003
Introduction © Ken Griffiths 2003
FIDUCIA PRESS
ISBN 0 946217 13 0
Printed in Great Britain by Doveton Press Ltd., Bristol

CONTENTS

Front cover: *Photograph of William Barnes, courtesy of Dorset County Museum.*

Back cover: *Collage from the mural 'Labour and History -the Struggle for Progress' 1986. Artists, Desmond Rochfort and Paul Butler. Courtesy of the TUC National Education Centre.*

Title Page: *This engraving by Thomas Bewick (1753-1828) reflects the hardships endured by the rural poor as a result of enclosures, the biggest single theft from the people in our history. William Barnes was a great admirer of Thomas Bewick's work and they had much in common. Both were inspired by a love of the countryside and were sensitive observers. They were also united in the warmth and tenderness of their natures.*

Page 6: *'Harvesters', an illustration by William Henry Pyne (1769 -1843).*

Page 8: *'Brean Down and Black Rock' at the mouth of the River Axe, Somerset. Engraved by William Barnes in 1829.*

Page 145: *'Haymaking', an illustration by William Henry Pyne.*

PREFACE

The publishers dedicate this reprint of 'Views of Labour and Gold' to Howard Utting of Bristol, for the use of his library and for his help at a most crucial time.

I have been a regular visitor to Dorset since childhood and was first introduced to the dialect poems of William Barnes (1801-1886) during my teenage years in the 1950s. Just prior to commencing my National Service I was fortunate enough to secure a copy of Thomas Hardy's *Select Poems of William Barnes* from a second hand bookshop in Bristol. Serving my time mostly overseas the book became a constant companion and led me to an appreciation of William Barnes and his works that has lasted until the present day.

My search for the works of William Barnes was rewarded by locating a copy of *Views of Labour and Gold*. This coincided with the start of my professional training. My first reading of *Labour and Gold* brought me to a realisation that here was a book that still had relevance to the modern reader. Over the years I have had occasion many times to refer to the wise and sensitive words of William Barnes contained in *Labour and Gold*. This supplied me with information and reassurance during my social work career and my political and union activities.

Sadly, in spite of much progress in the field of human endeavour since the mid-nineteenth century the world is still afflicted by many injustices and is certainly a more dangerous place. Poverty, the undermining of democratic processes and the willingness of transnational corporations to arm the most oppressive of regimes are all marks of global capitalism and must make this economic system the biggest single threat to world peace.

William Barnes had the deepest compassion for those dispossessed as a result of enclosures. One can imagine how he would have felt if he were alive today to witness the displacement of millions of people worldwide, due to economic policies forced on the weak by the powerful. The excuse given for this outrage is that 'there is no alternative to the globalised free market'. So how can a book on political and moral economy, written in 1859, be of encouragement to those who believe that the growing gap between the rich and poor need not be a fact of life and who believe that there can be no peace without justice? In my view *Labour and Gold* demonstrates that there are always alternatives and it also delivers a rebuke to those rich 'democracies' who are again embracing the concept of imperialism, the very antithesis of democracy. It was for these reasons that Roy Gallop (my partner in Fiducia Press) and I thought it appropriate and timely to make *Labour and Gold* the subject of a reprint.

It will be clear from my Introduction that my many readings of *Labour and Gold* have had an influence on me. Other readers of course may reach different conclusions to my own, but I am sure that they will still appreciate the scholarship and compassion of William

Barnes, the Dorset poet, priest and schoolmaster.

My Introduction includes a brief life of William Barnes, aimed particularly at readers who may be coming across him for the first time. My account of his life is of course no substitute for the three comprehensive biographies authored by Alan Chedzoy, Giles Dugdale and Trevor Hearl. Unfortunately these biographies are now out of print but can be obtained from some public libraries. The most recent of these biographies, by Alan Chedzoy, was published in 1985 and we can only hope that this very fine account of the life of William Barnes will one day be reprinted.

Also included in my Introduction are five dialect poems by William Barnes. For those unfamiliar with the Dorset dialect I have prepared a short glossary of Dorset words on page 146.

During a visit to the Dorset County Museum last year I came across recordings of a selection of the dialect poems of William Barnes, contained in a double CD. In my view this CD, *The Year Clock,* produced by Tim Lacock, is a must for those who are coming fresh to the beauty of the dialect poems. The poems are performed by Dorset speakers and reveal the very spirit of William Barnes, his compassion, his pride in the Dorset dialect and his love of the countryside.

The Foreword to this new publication of *Labour and Gold* is provided by Fr Andrew Phillips. He is the author of *The Rebirth of England and English: The Vision of William Barnes.* Fr Andrew is an Orthodox priest with a parish in Suffolk.

Ken Griffiths,
Fiducia Press
March 2003

FOREWORD

It is better to light a candle than to curse the darkness

English proverb

'A Poet? Nineteenth-century? Wrote in West Country dialect? William Barnes, you say? What possible relevance could he have today?' 'Well, I suppose people who like Dorset might be interested, or some local historian or Wessex regionalist, but as for me...'.

So goes the reasoning of many. It is false reasoning, for William Barnes was an extraordinary man, he was not just a brilliant poet, but also a linguist, a teacher, an inventor, a priest, a scientist, an artist, a musician, a historian and an economist. He is someone of whom not only Wessex should be proud, but all England, and indeed one whose vision is today of global importance.

The present book is, quite rightly, focused on William Barnes as a political economist. His 1859 work entitled, *Views of Labour and Gold* and reprinted here, is of profound relevance. After all, the whole of the nineteenth century was about the economic and therefore social and political developments resulting from the new technology of the Industrial Revolution. As for the twentieth century, its First World War was about the economic and territorial rivalries of different Imperialisms; its Second World War was between the ideologies of Nazism and Communism and that of the liberal democracies. And the end of that century was marked by the fearful Cold War between rival economic and political systems, which came close to destroying the world in a nuclear holocaust.

True, with the collapse of Communism, some spoke of the end of ideological battles. The 'West' was triumphant, they said, the free market and its unimpeded globalism had won. Oneworldism, the merging and even disappearance of all local identities was triumphant. In fact, however, globalism was only the new word for economic imperialism. You can change names, but the realities and truths are still there. In any case, globalism is not triumphant and that is being proved, as I write these lines, by the War that is now tearing apart Iraq and has divided the whole world. Ever since 9/11, the globalist MacWorld has been facing Jihad. The twenty-first century was born under the sign of opposition to the illusions of triumphant economic globalism.

William Barnes offers us neither the thesis of MacWorld, or its antithesis of Jihad. He offers us an alternative, a radical and prophetic vision of economic justice, in which work and money are both useful and fulfilling. Barnes' voice is that of David versus the Goliaths of modern injustice, the starving Third World versus the multi-billionaires of the transnationals and their political manipulations. Well over a hundred years before Schumacher, Barnes said that Small is Beautiful and that Local is Good.

Barnes expressed the soul of England, the True West, speaking prophetically against the powerbrokers in London, and beyond, in Brussels and Washington. He knew about 'Saxon Economics' and the true place of both labour and gold: both work and money are our servants, not our masters. Like all the old Bible, he spoke of the deception of capitalist Babylon and how its 'merchants were the great men of the earth; for by its sorceries were all nations deceived' (Revelation 18,23). Barnes had no illusions, as he wrote in his poem on sickness, *Zickness:*

> 'An' bags o' money at the end o' time
> Can't buy a soul, nor meake amends vor crime'.

It is our belief that the time is coming when Barnes' voice will be vindicated. From the roots and depths of English history and national consciousness, William Barnes' voice cries out to the spiritual and moral wilderness of contemporary economic globalism and proclaims that 'mercy and justice can meet together; righteousness and peace can kiss each other' (Psalm 85,10). William Barnes shows us that economic justice is possible- if only we are prepared to make the sacrifices to implement it.

Fr Andrew Phillips
Seekings House
25 March 2003

A Brief Life of William Barnes
and
Introduction to 'Views of Labour and Gold.'

William Barnes, one of the seven children of John, a small tenant farmer of modest means, was born at Bagber Common, near Sturminster Newton, on January 22nd 1801. His mother Grace died when he was just five years of age....

a woman of refined tastes and an inherent love of art and poetry. She only lived long enough to give her son the very first leanings towards art, which the boy showed in drawings on wall and floor, with chalks or anything which would mark, but the seed planted in the infantile mind grew after her death, as his memories of her strengthened.[1]

William's paternal Aunt Ann married Charles Roberts on August 8th 1780.[2] The couple appear to have performed a parental role in respect of William following his mother's death. Their love and influence, together with the daily presence of the Dorset countryside was probably crucial in the development of his talents and gentle nature.

William attended a Church of England endowed school in Sturminster Newton, leaving when he was thirteen years old. He took up employment locally, working as a clerk in the office of Thomas Henry Dashwood, a solicitor. It was said that William secured this position on account of his superb handwriting and drawing skills. His ambition however was to become an artist. On moving to Dorchester in 1818 to work for another solicitor, Thomas Coombes, he endeavoured to improve his skills as a wood and copper engraver, an interest he had acquired during schooldays. His desire to become a professional artist and engraver however remained an unfulfilled ambition. Later family commitments made economic considerations a priority and he was unable to receive the training to refine his natural talent and skills. William's raw talent however must have been recognised as over the years he accepted a fair number of engraving commissions. This not only gave him an opportunity to practice his craft but provided his family with much needed additional income.

In 1823 William became a schoolmaster, taking over an ailing school in Mere, Wiltshire. Its is evident then that his education did not cease on leaving school. Fired with a love of learning he devoted himself to the assimilation of knowledge. In this he was ably assisted by kindly and enlightened employers, also by friends and some of the local clergy, including a former headmaster of Dorchester

Grammar School, the Rev. Henry John Richman. A willing pupil William embraced the study of Greek and Latin. His field of study also extended to drawing, engraving, music and mathematics.

The Rev. Richman was a competent and sensitive educator who was totally opposed to corporal punishment in his establishment, an enlightened view at the beginning of the nineteenth century. Giving generously of his time he instructed William in the technique and art of poetry, a gift that combined with William's inspirational talent has been shared with countless numbers of poetry lovers over many generations. That the Rev. Richman was influential in William's social and educational development cannot be doubted. It is also likely that William's religious convictions began to take shape during this period. I believe that his passion for education partly stemmed from the help he received during his adolescence, becoming aware of the liberating effect that a fund of general knowledge can have. Following the example of the Rev. Richman his desire to share knowledge became vocational and this continued long after his retirement as a schoolmaster in 1862.

The importance of books during William's nine years of part time study must surely be the source of his poem *Learning*, [3] one verse being particularly poignant....

> Books that purify the thought,
> Spirits of the learned dead,
> Teachers of the little taught,
> Comforters when friends have fled.

William was fortunate that in his formative years he lived close to a neighbour, Jemmy Jenkins, who had a collection of over two hundred books. It appears that Jemmy performed the function of local sage and was regarded with somewhat fearful respect by the community. Included in his library were books on Astronomy, Astrology and Magic, a fascinating mixture to an imaginative child. John Barnes did not approve of his son's frequent visits to the home of Jemmy Jenkins but the lure of so many books was too hard for William to resist.

Whatever anxieties William may have felt when he arrived at Mere he was probably quietly confident that his studies had prepared him sufficiently well enough to cope with his new career. He had to start his school almost from scratch. It was housed in a loft above the Market House, situated in the town centre. Although

William took naturally to teaching his gentle and retiring nature must have been a handicap at first. His abilities and passion for education however were soon asserted and his simple and gentle approach to teaching and discipline became strengths.

Whilst at Mere William continued to further his own education. This laid the foundation for his many accomplishments in later life. He engraved in wood and copper, wrote poetry, learned languages and studied their history. Throughout his life he was to remain steadfast in the belief that Anglo-Saxon was sufficiently word rich for the English language to have no need of imports from other sources. It was at Mere that William first wrote poems in the Dorset dialect. His first published books, *Poetical Pieces* and *Orra: A Lapland Tale* were published prior to his move from Dorchester.[4] These were written in National English.

In 1827 William moved his school within Mere to Chantry House, near the parish church of St Michael. In the same year and only one month after taking up residence he married Julia Miles. They had first met, not by introduction but by chance in Dorchester when William was eighteen years of age; Julia was two years younger. Contemporary accounts, their letters and William's poems reveal that this was a love at first sight experience, a love that lasted throughout their lives.

Julia and her family had moved from Dorchester to Nailsea, Somerset, in 1825 and it was here that William and Julia were married, at the parish church of the Holy Trinity. From the very beginning of the marriage Julia performed an active and vital role in the management of the new school, a mixed establishment of boarders.

The environment of Chantry House allowed William to restore his links with his former rustic life. Having the humility never to deny his humble origins he revelled in the cultivation of his garden. No task was too menial for him. Growing his own produce however was not just for pleasure or out of economic necessity. It is likely that this was a practical protest against the spread of enclosures that were wreaking havoc on the lives of rural workers and their families. It is possible also that William's involvement with husbandry and craft skills was an attempt to propagate, by example, the desirability of self-sufficiency. He felt that this would ensure that workers had time to engage in meaningful pursuits of their choice and that this would improve the quality of their lives.

William deplored the advance of intensive farming methods, which quickly became a feature of enclosure. He had a countryman's instinct that in the long term such methods could only compromise good husbandry. William also feared the breakdown of the rural way of life he was familiar with, the preservation of which he associated with a degree of independence for the rural labour force. The withdrawal of customary rights of common would make day labourers of many, a condition amounting to wage slavery and insecurity.

William's compassion for the rural poor is reflected not only in his poems but in the articles he wrote for the *Dorset County Chronicle and Somerset Gazette.*

The effects of enclosure are sensitively portrayed by William in his dialect poem *The Common a-Took in* and in his pastoral dialogue poem of the same name.[5] The latter poem depicts a conversation between Thomas and John that captures not only the insecurity of agricultural workers during this period but their bewilderment at the changes taking place.

Eclogue: The Common a-Took in

THOMAS AN' JOHN

THOMAS
Good morn t'ye, John. How b'ye? how b'ye?
Zoo you be gwaïn to market, I do zee.
Why, you be quite a-lwoaded wi' your geese.

JOHN
Ees, Thomas, ees.
Why, I'm a-gettèn rid ov ev'ry goose
An' goslèn I've a-got: an' what is woose,
I fear that I must zell my little cow.

THOMAS
How zoo, then, John? Why, what's the matter now?
What, can't ye get along? B'ye run a-ground?
An' can't paÿ twenty shillèns vor a pound?
What, can't ye put a lwoaf on shelf?

JOHN

Ees, now;

But I do fear I shan't 'ithout my cow.

No; they do meän to teäke the moor in, I do hear,

An' 'twill be soon begun upon;

Zoo I must zell my bit o' stock to-year,

Because they woon't have any groun' to run upon.

THOMAS

Why, what d'ye tell o'? I be very zorry

To hear what they be gwaïn about;

But yet I s'pose there'll be a 'lotment vor ye,

When they do come to make it out.

JOHN

No; not vor me, I fear. An' if there should,

Why 'twoulden be so handy as 'tis now;

Vor 'tis the common that do do me good,

The run vor my vew geese, or vor my cow.

THOMAS

Ees, that's the job; why 'tis a handy thing

To have a bit o' common, I do know,

To put a little cow upon in Spring,

The while woone's bit ov orcha'd grass do grow.

JOHN

Aye, that's the thing, you zee. Now I do mow

My bit o' grass, an' meäke a little rick;

An' in the zummer, while do grow,

My cow do run in common vor to pick

A bleäde or two o'grass, if she can vind em,

Vor tother cattle don't leäve much behind em.

Zoo in the evenèn, we do put a lock

O' nice fresh grass avore the wicket;

An' she do come at vive or zix o'clock,

As constant as the zun, to pick it.

An' then , bezides the cow, why we do let

Our geese run out among the emmet hills;

An' then when we do pluck em, we do get

Vor zeäle zome veathers an' zome quills;

An' in the winter we do fat em well,

An' car em to the market vor to zell
To gentlevo'ks, vor we don't oft avvword
To put a goose a-top ov ouer bwoard;
But we do get our feäst, - vor we be eäble
To clap the giblets up a-top o' teäble.

THOMAS
An' I don't know o' many better things,
Than geese's heads and gizzards, lags an' wings.

JOHN
An' then, when I ha' nothèn else to do,
Why I can teäke my hook an' gloves, an' goo
To cut a lot o' vuzz and briars
Vor hetèn ovens, or vor lightèn viers.
An' when the children be too young to eärn
A penny, they can g'out in zunny weather,
An' run about, an' get together
A bag o' cow-dung vor to burn.

THOMAS
'Tis handy to live near a common;
But I've a-zeed, an' I've a-zaid,
That if a poor man got a bit o' bread,
They'll try to teäke it vrom en.
But I wer twold back tother day,
That they be got into a way
O' lettèn bits o' groun' out to the poor.

JOHN
Well, I do hope 'tis true, I'm sure;
An' I do hope that they will do it here,
Or I must goo to workhouse, I do fear.

This poem, William's first in the Dorset dialect to be published, appeared in the *Dorset County Chronicle* on January 2nd 1834.

William's compassion for the rural poor is well known, but his solutions to relieve their poverty, to improve their working conditions and to restore their dignity were anything but radical. He preferred reform within what was left of the old social framework. One of William's solutions to relieve the hardships being experienced by agricultural labourers and rural artisans was for the provision of allotments, a reasonable enough proposal. He reasoned that this could offset some of the worse effects of enclosure, bringing some security to workers and limiting unrest, thus restoring stability to the community. Those with political and economic power however had a different agenda. The existence of a labour force that was less exploitable would interfere with their plans for wealth creation. Agricultural workers 'surplus to requirements' could be accommodated within the ever growing manufacturing industries that would eventually lead to massive urban conurbations.

William's second dialect poem to be published, *Eclogue: The 'Lotments* [6] gives an indication why he felt that widespread allotment provision would be an effective and peaceful response to injustice. This proposal could be considered an inadequate, even quaint response to a problem of such massive proportions, but even in our own time there have been serious attempts to achieve local self-sufficiency, not only for health and environmental reasons but as a political statement, an antidote to the exploitative and dangerous nature of agribusiness.

Eclogue: The 'Lotments

JOHN AND RICHARD

JOHN
Zoo you be in your groun' then , I do zee,
A-workèn and a-zingèn lik' a bee.
How do it answer? What d'ye think about it?
D'ye think 'tis better wi' it than without it?
A-reck'nèn rent, an' time, an' zeed to stock it,
D'ye think that you be any thing in pocket?

RICHARD
O, 'tis a goodish help to woone, I'm sure o't.
If I had not a-got it, my poor bwones
Would now ha' eäch'd a-crakèn stwones
Upon the road; I wish I had zome mwore o't.

JOHN
I wish the girt woones had a-got the greäce
To let out land lik this in ouer pleäce;
But I do fear there'll never be nwone vor us,

An I can't tell whatever we shall do:
We be a most a-starvèn, an' we'd goo
To 'merica, if we'd enough to car us.

RICHARD

Why 'twer the squire, good now! A worthy man,
That vu'st brought into ouer pleäce the plan;
He zaid he'd let a vew odd eäcres
O' land to us poor leäb'rèn men;
An' faïth, he had enough o' teäkers
Vor that, an' twice so much ageän.
Zoo I took zome here, near my hovel,
To exercise my speäde an' shovel;
An' what wi' dungèn, diggèn up, an' zeedèn,
A-thinnèn, cleänèn, howèn up an' weedèn,
I, an' the biggest o' the childern too,
Do always vind some useful jobs to do.

JOHN

Aye, wi' a bit o' ground, if woone got any,
Woone's bwoys can soon get out an' eärn a penny;
An' then, by workèn, they do learn the vaster
The way to do things when they have a meäster;
Vor woone must know a deäl about the land
Bevore woone's fit to lend a useful hand,
In geärden or a-vield upon a farm.

RICHARD

An' then the work do keep em out o' harm;
Vor vo'ks that don't do nothèn wull be vound
Soon doen woorse than nothèn, I'll be bound.
But as vor me, d'ye zee, wi' theäse here bit
O' land, why I have ev'ry thing a'mwost:
Vor I can fatten vowels vor the spit,
Or zell a good fat goose or two to rwoast;
An' have my beäns or cabbage, greens or grass,
Or bit o' wheat, or, sich my happy feäte is,
That I can keep a little cow, or ass,
An' a vew pigs to eat the little teäties.

JOHN
An' when your pig's a-fatted pretty well
Wi' teäties, or wi' barley an' some bran,
Why you've a-got zome vlitches vor to zell,
Or hang in chimney-corner, if you can.

RICHARD
Aye, that's the thing; an' when the pig do die,
We got a lot ov offal vor to fry,
An' netlèns vor to bwoil; or put the blood in,
An' meäke a meal or two o' good black-pudden.

JOHN
I'd keep myzelf from parish, I'd be bound,
If I could get a little patch o' ground.

Another pastoral dialect poem, *Rusticas Res Politicas Animadvertens: The New Poor Laws* reflects the fears and anxieties of rural workers deprived of customary rights.

William's poems and articles published in the 1820s and 1830s, some relating to the plight of the rural poor, were published anonymously. His reason for this may have been influenced by the times he was living through. Drawing attention to the defects of a harsh and sometimes corrupt political and social system carried with it certain dangers, as the six Tolpuddle Martyrs [7] found out to their cost in 1834. In their particular case the Statute Book was trawled to find an Act that could be stretched and manipulated to force the men (and justice) into exile. It is unlikely that William would have been under any real threat from the authorities but anonymity could have been the simple precaution of a family man in troubled times.

There may of course have been another reason for anonymity. William had not achieved his high level of education using academic channels. Largely self taught, albeit with vital assistance at times, his self esteem may have been somewhat shaky. William was already in middle age when his achievements were beginning to be recognised and even then certain literary and establishment figures could only see his modest upbringing and self taught status. This must surely have been the reason why, in 1846, his application to become headmaster of Hardyes', the Dorchester Grammar School was rejected, this at a time when William was enjoying national recognition as a poet and his school renowned for its excellence. He had not come into his full confidence in the 1830s and probably felt disinclined to test himself against academics unless under the cloak of anonymity.

William, with his pacifist nature became alarmed at any community disorder and wrote a pastoral poem, *The Unioners*,[8] published in the *Dorset County Chronicle* on December 6th 1838. This work shows that he had a good grasp of why workers were agitating for political rights, but the poem still appeals for calm and for workers to put their trust in traditional ways. William, who would always go kindly with people had a simple faith in his God and truly believed that an independent pastoral life, lived under the guidance of a caring squirearchy was the ideal. His views of course clashed head on with the growth of gross capitalism, a system that gave no quarter in the drive for profits. The workers, experiencing the fracture of traditional social structures and whose basic needs were immediate and having no redress for their legitimate grievances began to organise to protect their customary rights. Some took to wrecking property to bring attention to the violence of poverty.[9] Others agitated for political rights through the Union and Chartist movements. William of course had much in common with the Chartists, something he did not fully appreciate at the time. He was later to express concerns that in *The Unioners* he had misunderstood their just motives.

In middle age William did become more political. His writings were no longer published anonymously and he engaged in a high profile programme of free lectures to the working class, often with a political content. These lectures were used as the basis of his book on political and moral economy, *Views of Labour and Gold,* published in 1859.

William and Julia lived together in Mere for eight happy years. Three of their seven children were born during this time; Laura in 1828, Julia in 1832 and Julius in 1834.

In 1835 the Barnes family left Mere to take up residence in Dorchester. William set up a day and boarding school in Durngate Street. Julia not only continued to act as administrator but also carried out many of the practical tasks associated with the smooth running of an educational establishment.

It was here that tragedy struck the family. In 1837 Julius Barnes died, aged just three years. He was buried in All Saints churchyard, Dorchester. The devastating impact that the death of Julius had on this sensitive family can easily be imagined. It seems that William and Julia attempted to relieve their pain by keeping their grief private. They made fewer and fewer references to Julius in public, probably to spare themselves further hurt. In this way they were better able to manage their grief and move on. William however wrote several poems in memory of Julius, including *The Mother's Dream, For a Child Lost, The Turnstile* and *Our Little Boy.*

Lucy Barnes was born on January 21st 1837, a few months before the death of Julius. Lucy was to write a biography of her father, published in 1887.

On January 22nd 1838 William and Julia moved home and school to 17, South Street, Dorchester. Although practical considerations probably dictated the move it is also likely that their decision was partly influenced by the association of the Durngate Street establishment with the death of their son. Whether the move was considered by William and Julia as a fresh start or not the result was the establishment of an excellent educational facility that was to enjoy a fine reputation for many years. A wide range of subjects were offered over and above the usual basic subjects. This ensured choice as well as stimulation and it is not surprising that many of William's pupils went on to achieve positions of eminence in the Victorian establishment.

William believed that drudgery was contrary to a well-balanced and happy life. He strived to make the teaching of all subjects as appealing as possible and knew the value of including the Arts and Games in the curriculum. Pupils also had the advantage of a teacher with linguistic skills (he was competent in many languages, including French, Hindustani, Italian, Persian and Welsh).

William recalled the joys of his countryside childhood in some of his poems. It may well be that he wished to share these joys with his pupils. Just two lines from his poem *Rustic Childhood* [10] may reveal the ethos of his school.....

> We spent in woodland shades our day
> In cheerful work and happy play

We can only guess at the long-term gains to society if the early state system of education had embraced William's educational philosophy and teaching methods. In my view the gains would have been considerable. Unfortunately the state had a different agenda and the system that developed, often administered under harsh regimes did little to help children realise their full potential.

The introduction of the comprehensive system of education in the 1960s did much to redress the balance. Sadly and inexplicably this now well tried and tested facility, staffed by committed but now demoralised teachers is under threat. Specialist schools and creeping selection will again define education in its narrowest sense. William of course knew very well the distinct difference between schooling and education, the tyranny of the former and the liberating effect of the latter.

Between 1838 and 1843 Julia gave birth to three more children; Isabel in 1839, William Miles in 1840 and Egbert in 1843.

Although William gave priority to his teaching vocation he still found time to continue his studies. His interests extended to philology, archaeology, music (he was a musician and composer as well as a fine singer), early British history, engraving and of course poetry. He continued to write articles for the prominent magazines of the day including *The Reader* and *Macmillan's Magazine.*

William's school was considered by many to be a prestigious Academy. A move to larger premises at 40, South Street, Dorchester was undertaken in 1847 to accommodate the ever growing number of pupils. The school functioned here until its closure in 1862.

It was at Mere that William began writing textbooks for use in schools. This activity gave him the confidence and experience so essential in the writing of his major works. In 1840 William's *An investigation of the Laws of Case in Language* was published. *An Arithmetical and Commercial Dictionary* was published in the same year. 1842 saw the publication of *The Elements of English Grammar.*

The publication of William's *Poems of Rural Life in the Dorset Dialect* in 1844 strengthened his reputation as a sensitive and sincere poet. It was also to bring him national recognition. In this he was aided by the patronage of Caroline Norton, the writer and reformer. At first glance it would appear that William and Caroline had little in common, separated as they were by origins and class. On closer examination however it is soon revealed that they shared a love of poetry, learning and a desire for social justice. Both were passionate in their beliefs, Caroline in her campaigns for women's rights and the abolition of child labour, William in his opposition to enclosure and intensive farming. Their methods of achieving their aims though were very different. Caroline was robust in her attacks on a legal system that discriminated against women and denied them justice in relation to infant custody and property rights. A victim of her husband's physical and mental cruelty and receiving no help from the courts she directed her talents and passion into the writing of vigorous pamphlets to improve the legal status and human rights of women. Her spirited campaigns, with the support of public opinion were instrumental in changing the law on infant custody (1839) and marriage and divorce (1857). Caroline's *English Laws for Women* was probably her most influential work.

William tried to influence by example and humility, his gentleness of nature and perhaps his religious beliefs dictating this course of action.

Discussions between William and Caroline must have been both stimulating and satisfying. William's breadth of learning, his courtesy and sensitivity was in marked contrast to the dissolute nature of Caroline's husband. It is likely that her admiration for William's poetry gave a boost to his general level of confidence. Caroline could also have stirred in William the beginnings of political awareness, paving the way for his *'Labour and Gold'* lectures. It is clear that Caroline influenced William's decision to write poems in National English, a selection being published in 1846 *(Poems Partly of Rural Life in National English)*. William's poems in National English are sometimes compared unfavourably to his dialect poems. It is true that his talent, virtues and imagination are more easily recognisable in his dialect poems. However, in my view many examples of skilful and sensitive compositions can be found in his National English collections.

When *Poems of Rural Life in the Dorset Dialect* was published William was half way through a course of study that would eventually culminate in the award of a Bachelor degree of Divinity in 1850. William's interest in religion had a long history and it is no surprise that in 1837 he commenced his formal religious training. This was made possible by enrolling on a ten year course of part time study administered by St John's College, Cambridge. William was an active layman of St Peter's Church, Dorchester. He carried out duties not only of churchwarden but also of sick visitor, a position he was most suitably qualified to hold.

William was ordained deacon in 1847 and appointed curate of Whitcombe Church, two miles south east of Dorchester. He was ordained priest in 1848. As this appointment was not a full time position he was still able to devote time to his teaching vocation and his other interests. Whitcombe Church is part twelfth century, but has Saxon origins. By good fortune the church still retains some medieval wall paintings and is also noteworthy as the location where William preached his first and last sermons of his ministry. Whitcombe Church is now cared for by the Churches Conservation Trust and is open to the public.

In the same year as his ordination as Deacon William moved his family and school into larger premises at 40, South Street, Dorchester. During the next four years the school was to reach the pinnacle of its success and reputation.

The period 1840 to 1850 was a decade not only of academic achievement for William but of active involvement in the life of the community. His concern on hearing that the intended route of the new railway system was to pass through sites of historic importance prompted him to take action to preserve these unique links with our past. With a quiet fortitude and with the help of like minded supporters he succeeded in having the offending lines diverted. We really do owe William and his supporters a debt of gratitude for preserving the remains that are so familiar to us now. Indeed one would find it very difficult to imagine Dorchester without the Maumbury Rings which still provides a social amenity for many families during the spring and summer months. In 1845 William was instrumental in the founding of the Dorset County Museum. This facility is still the focus of much cultural activity in the County.

During the 1840s William continued engraving, illustrating text books he wrote for use in his school. His *The Elements of Linear Perspective and the Projection of Shadows* (1842) is illustrated by diagrams of his own creation, produced from wood-blocks. Although it is likely that by this time he had given up all hope of becoming a professional artist it is evident that he still enjoyed working in this particular craft form.

1846 saw the publication of *Poems Partly of Rural Life in National English.* A fruitful decade for William ended with the publication of *Se Gefylsta (The Helper): An Anglo-Saxon Delectus.* Also in 1849 he wrote a series of articles for the *Poole and Dorset Herald* under the title *Humilus Domus: Some thoughts on the Abodes, Life and Social Conditions of the Poor, Especially in Dorsetshire.*These articles reveal that Williams's social awareness was taking on a political dimension, a trend that was to continue until he had formulated his own social, economic and political philosophy. The advent of the new decade saw the

Barnes family as happy and prosperous. This tranquillity however was shattered in 1852 by the death from cancer of his much loved wife. William's scrapbook for 1852 contains this entry:

June 21 A day of sorrow and beginning of a chain of
         sorrows - At half after eleven o'clock in
         the morning, my great loss.[11]

The devastating circumstance of Julia's death drove the family into the vale of tears. William's reference to the 'beginning of a chain of sorrows' in his diary entry reveals his awareness that his grief would be long lasting. Ill-health marked the passage of the next two years and in 1854 he contracted rheumatic fever, a condition which severely restricted the effective use of his hands, a cruel blow for an artist. It is possible that the root cause of William's ill-health was a prolonged grief reaction, a condition that can have adverse effects on the immune system. William's struggle to regain his health was assisted by his vocational spirit and this was eventually to overcome his loss. His memories and feelings for Julia however remained with him until his death, as is revealed in the many elegies he wrote to her. In *The Wife a-Lost*,[12] published six years after Julia's death we get more than a glimpse of the deep love they shared.

The Wife a-Lost

Since I noo mwore do zee your feäce,
Up steäirs or down below,
I'll zit me in the lwonesome pleäce,
Where flat-bough'd beech do grow;
Below the beeches' bough, my love,
Where you did never come,
An' I don't look to meet ye now,
As I do look at hwome.

Since you noo mwore be at my zide,
In walks in zummer het,
I'll goo alwone where mist do ride,
Drough trees a-drippèn wet;
Below the raïn-wet bough, my love,
Where you did never come,
An' I don't grieve to miss ye now,
As I do grieve at hwome.

Since now bezide my dinner-bwoard
Your vaïce do never sound,
I'll eat the bit I can avword,
A-vield upon the ground;
Below the darksome bough, my love,
Where you did never dine,
An' I don't grieve to miss ye now,
As I at hwome do pine.

Since I do miss your vaïce an' feäce
In praÿer at eventide,
I'll praÿ wi' woone sad vaïce vor greäce
To goo where you do bide;
Above the tree an' bough, my love,
Where you be gone avore,
An' be a-waïtèn vor me now,
To come vor evermwore.

Julia was buried in St Peter's churchyard, Dorchester. Although a statue of William Barnes now stands on this site there is no memorial or marker to Julia. There is an injustice here when one considers the vital role played by Julia in running the schools, caring for her family and supporting William in all his endeavours. Julia's presence in his life allowed his talents to flourish and enabled many of his works to see the light of day. Without her William would not have had the time to pursue the study of such a wide range of subjects or to provide so wide a curriculum that so distinguished his school from the mainstream. I am reminded of the fine statue of Florence Nightingale in London, part of a feature to commemorate the Crimean War. Missing from the feature is a statue of the nurse Mary Seacole.[13] In other words the feature tells only half the story. So it is with William and Julia. Without a fitting memorial to Julia her husband must stand in isolation.

Not only the family was affected by Julia's death. The school was sorely disadvantaged also. The guiding hand that so admirably assisted William in his often radical approach to education could not be replaced. William's daughters, Laura and Julia, rallied round their father to make positive efforts to ensure that the school continued to function effectively. It became apparent however that William no longer had the physical and mental energy to fulfil his influential role so important to the ethos of the school. A gradual decline in standards and reputation occurred resulting in a fall in pupil numbers. There was however a glimpse, perhaps just a flash of the school's former excellence when in 1862 one of its pupils, Thomas Talbort achieved first place in the Indian Civil Service Examination. The results were announced on June 20th, the day the school closed.

It was typical of William that at the time of his deepest distress the plight of the poor was still of concern to him. Holding the view that education was of prime importance in achieving for the working class a life free from hardship and exploitation he continued his programme of free lectures that he had commenced in 1851. He lectured on a variety of subjects and also gave poetry readings, often in the Dorset dialect. This move into adult education was inspired by his passion for service and may in the end have been therapeutic.

1859 saw the publication of William's book on political and moral economy, *Views of Labour and Gold.* 1859 also saw the publication of William's second collection of poems in the Dorset dialect, *Hwomely Rhymes.* In 1862 William gave up the struggle to save his ailing school and it closed in June. Earlier in the year he was offered the living of Winterborne Came by Captain Seymour Dawson Damer, a former pupil. William took up residence at the rectory and thus, at the age of sixty one commenced his new career as a country parson. In a sense he had been preparing for this all his life. It was a just reward for a lifetime of service to the community. The next twenty four years were ones of security and contentment, but not of retirement. As well as carrying out his duties as parish priest he continued to write poetry and books on philology. Between 1862 and 1886, the year of his death his published works included *Poems of Rural Life in the Dorset Dialect: Third Collection; Poems of Rural Life in Common English; Early England and the Saxon-English; An Outline of English Speech-Craft;* an omnibus edition of his three collections of poems in the Dorset dialect; *Ruth, A Short Drama* and *A Glossary of the Dorset Dialect.* In 1867 William gave written evidence to the *Royal Commission on Employment of Children, Young Persons and Women in Agriculture.*

William also continued his practice of writing articles for magazines. His lectures and poetry readings he considered to be an important part of his life and only ill-health brought an end to this activity. Even so he was eighty years old when he gave his last lecture. This volume of work would not have been considered by William as a chore, it was his pleasure, what he himself would have described as 'happy labour'. William was generous in his acceptance of visitors who wished to pay their respects, perhaps even to learn something from him. The diarist the Rev.

Francis Kilvert describes a visit he made to William in 1874....

I was immediately struck by the beauty and grandeur of his head. It was an Apostolic head, bald and venerable, and the long soft silvery hair flowed on his shoulders and a long white beard fell upon his breast. His face was handsome and striking, keen yet benevolent, the finely pencilled eyebrows still dark and a beautiful benevolent loving look lighted up his fine dark blue eyes when they rested upon you. He is a very remarkable and a very remarkable-looking man, half hermit, half enchanter. The Poet seemed pleased with my visit and gratified that I had come such a long way to see him. I told him I had for many years known him through his writings and had long wished to thank him in person for the many happy hours his poems had given me. He smiled and said he was very glad if he had given me any pleasure. Frequently stroking his face and his venerable white beard the Poet told me he had composed his poems chiefly in the evening as a relaxation from the day's work when he kept a school in Dorchester....[14]

William's friend Thomas Hardy who lived nearby at Max Gate was of course a frequent visitor and was to write *The Last Signal*, a memoriam to his fellow poet. Fittingly William's last poem was in the Dorset dialect, *The Geäte a-Vallen to,* dictated in 1885. William died on October 7th 1886 at the rectory. His funeral was modest for a man who had given such a loving and comprehensive service to the community but this was in keeping with his humility, which was such a feature of his life. This modest and sweet tempered man, whose gentleness of nature was often remarked upon was laid to rest by his family and the poets Thomas Hardy and Francis Palgrave. In attendance also were his parishioners, both adults and children, who above all knew his true worth. Throughout William's long and fruitful life he was always mindful of the disadvantaged and those who suffered through the avarice and insensitivity of the powerful. His compassionate observations of the human condition are clearly revealed in his poem *The Love Child.*[15]

The Love Child

Where the bridge out at Woodley did stride,
Wi' his wide arches' cool sheäded bow,
Up above the clear brook that did slide
By the poppies, befoam'd white as snow:
As the gil'cups did quiver among
The white deäisies, a-spread in a sheet,
There a quick-trippen maïd come along, -
Aye, a girl wi' her light-steppen veet.
An' she cried 'I do praÿ, is the road

Out to Lincham on here, by the meäd?'
An' 'oh! ees, 'I meäde answer, an' show'd
Her the way it would turn an' would leäd:
'Goo along by the beech in the nook,
Where the childern do plaÿ in the cool,
To the steppen stwones over the brook, -
Aye, the grey blocks o' rock at the pool.'

'Then you don't seem a-born an' a-bred,'
I spoke up, 'at a place her about;'
An' she answer'd wi' cheäks up so red
As a pi'ny but leäte a-come out,
'No, I liv'd wi' my uncle that died
Back in Eäpril, an' now I'm a-come
Here to Ham, to my mother, to bide, -
Aye, to her house to vind a new hwome.'

I'm asheämed that I wanted to know
Any mwore ov her childhood or life,
But then, why should so feäir a child grow
Where noo father did bide wi' his wife;
Then wi' blushes ov zunrisèn morn,
She replied that 'it midden be known
Oh! they zent me away to be born,
Aye, they hid me when zome would be shown.'

Oh! it meäde me a'most teary-ey'd,
An' I vound I a'most could ha' groan'd -
What! So winnen, an' still cast azide -
What! So lovely, an' not to be own'd;
Oh! a God-gift a-treated wi' scorn,
Oh! a child that a squier should own;
An' to zend her away to be born! -
Aye, to hide her where others be shown!

William is best remembered for his poetry. Those who derived pleasure, perhaps even guidance from his poems, have, over the years kept the fruits of his talents alive. But what of his other works? Many would now have little appeal except to scholars and students of history, who of course would be appreciative of William's scholarship.

One book however stands out as being meaningful to the modern reader. In my view *Labour and Gold* is more than a contemporary account of mid-nineteenth century economics and William's well thought out suggestions on how to achieve social justice for the people. One can detect a sense of alarm in his writing and not a little prophecy. He was well aware that although the growth of unregulated capitalism could lead to prosperity for a few, it could also bring misery to many more. William's concern for the poor extended beyond these shores. He was appalled at the catastrophic effects that imperial capitalism was having on the peoples of the world and argued for alternatives to such a grossly unfair and sometimes cruel economic system.

William's views made him unpopular in certain quarters of society, a situation familiar today to those who propagate alternatives to the free market, as practised by the all powerful global corporations.

During his lifetime William saw the painfully slow extension of the franchise and probably came to the correct conclusion that it would be many years before democracy had any impact on life improvement for the masses. Even in 1885, just one year before his death only 60% of men were entitled to vote. Women were excluded altogether. *Labour and Gold,* coupled with his simple Christian message that neighbour should have regard for neighbour was William's contribution in the struggle to achieve for people a happy and well balanced life without the need for conflict. William lived his beliefs, encouraging people by example to come to an understanding that true wealth is life itself. However, for those suffering under often unendurable economic and social burdens the concept of democracy appeared to offer a solution to their problems. There is of course truth in that, but just as William's views were ignored by the powerful so has our long fought for democracy been neutralised from the same source.

In Britian, after much struggle and over a painfully long period of time, a working democracy became a reality in 1928 when women secured the vote on the same terms as men. By the mid to late 1940s new legislation in education, health, welfare, transport, industry and industrial relations was to bring a growing sense of security to the community.

Incredibly in the 21st century these bedrock provisions are under threat. There has been a slow decline in social democracy since 1979. This decline has accelerated since 1997. During the 1990s the Labour party was hijacked by a gang of free marketeers, who, by posing as the opposite when in opposition, achieved political power. They have since cut a swathe through civil liberties and blatantly attempted to control the media. The common good has taken second place to the needs of global corporations. There is a move towards international trade agreements that once again will render citizens powerless to protect their interests, perhaps their very lives. The corporate marauders, aided and abetted by the International Monetary Fund, the World Trade Organisation, the World Bank and insecure or approving governments, including our own, are despoiling the world and its peoples in the ruthless pursuit of power and profits. The seamless transition from a Conservative government to a Labour government left many people who had a belief in the common good feeling betrayed, bewildered and with a contempt for politics. In the 2001 election the electorate became aware that they had been robbed of an expected choice of social and economic systems. The concentration by the media on the three major parties, all favouring the free market, had the effect of squeezing out the views of the smaller parties. New Labour were returned to office by securing the votes of just one in four of the eligible electorate.

Politicians still continue the practice of scapegoating vulnerable groups as a cover for oppressive policies or to divert attention from problems that arise as a result of an adherence to an economic system that favours the de-regulation of business. Aware that this could provoke a reaction they re-regulate the people through criminal 'justice' and anti-union legislation, making just and legitimate protest more and more difficult. This situation would be only too familiar to those opposing tyranny in William's time.

In *Labour and Gold* William expressed his hope for a better world and gave guidelines on how this could be achieved. Indeed, a reader will come to a realisation that a number of William's suggestions to improve the quality of life of the people were eventually to pass into legislation. William was making an appeal for an appreciation of other peoples cultures, to be aware of the uniqueness and joy of diversity and to resist the imposing of one culture on another. Sadly, for some the of the peoples he referred to the worst was yet to come, European imperialism being unleashed on unsuspecting communities with all its force during the late nineteenth and early twentieth centuries.

When *Labour and Gold* was published in 1859 the United States of America was still a partial slave economy and was accelerating the continental drive westward that was to devastate the lives of the remaining indigenous population. William deplored slavery and exploitation and it is reasonable to assume that he was able to predict America's imperial ambitions. By the mid-twentieth century the USA had superseded Britain as the world's most powerful imperialist nation, a position it still holds.

The interference by the political, economic and military wings of the US establishment in the affairs of other (mostly poor) nations is the complete antithesis of William's concept of moral and political economics. America's protection of transnational corporations is responsible for much (but not of course all) of the inequality that is prevalent in the world today, including ironically a vast number of American citizens. Family incomes in the United States have remained static in real terms since the 1970s, wages being among the lowest of the G-7 nations.[16] 45 million people are without health insurance and 12% of the population live below the poverty line.[17] This situation occurs in the world's richest country because the American establishment and the transnational corporations collude with each other to preserve the capitalist system. No quarter is given, even to American citizens if profits are at stake. Less than 1% of the population own more than 38% of US wealth.[18]

A comment by William in *Labour and Gold* under the chapter 'True Wealth' is as valid today as it was in 1859.

.....the more common kinds of worldly wealth are of uncertain effect, though the peace of a community is none the safer for a greater inequality of wealth, such that one class may be over-rich to wanton luxury, while another are poor to naked hunger.[19]

William and the early pioneers of democracy would be both saddened and horrified to learn of today's growing gap between the rich and poor, this offence taking place in a Britain that has the world's fourth strongest economy. Corporate interests have proved more powerful than William's gentle and logical pleas, and certainly more powerful than our democracy that has been neutered by corporate propaganda. The capitalist media spreads this propaganda throughout the world which assists the transnational corporations in their drive to control all the world's natural resources, from oil to water. As worrying is global capitalism's gradual encroachment into the areas of health and welfare. More worrying, perhaps even sinister is the privatisation of educational services.

Transnational corporations exploit by offering to aid, to bandage ailing economies. Too late the people come to an understanding that the dressing is infected, bringing millions to a state of impoverishment and dependency. Poverty, the undermining of democratic processes and the willingness of transnational corporations to arm the most oppressive of regimes are all marks of global capitalism and must make this economic system the biggest single threat to world peace.

William was aware of the unjust nature of imperialism as is revealed in a sermon he delivered at St. Peter's church, Dorchester, at the time of the Indian Mutiny.[20] It is apparent that William was making an appeal to those in authority to come to an understanding as to why this major conflict arose and to measure their response. He gave his view that....

Justice is stronger for good than wild revenge and the spirit of Christ is stronger than both.

This appeal to love and reason could just as well be put to the advocates of the new imperialism, and should be, before they unleash further horrors on the world.

Parliamentary democracy has been so abused by politicians that it is now dying, but in my view there will be a resurgence of democracy outside parliament that will be more in keeping with the aims of its early advocates. Expressions of this democracy will have more legitimacy than our present system that for all practical purposes limits the peoples involvement in the process to voting just once every four or five years. Perhaps the first step in recovering democracy from the politicians, before they distort it beyond all recognition is by a return to the founding principles of social democracy. Although William never came to a full understanding of the role of democracy in society his writings in *Labour and Gold* proved the need for one. Education and experience, as always, can be liberating and what better place to start than by tapping into the writings of a great educator blessed with the gift of humility. The following extract from *Labour and Gold,* written in 1859 is a fair definition of today's global capitalism.

Another feeling allied to that of miserliness is the money-making mind, which looks on the works of God or the pursuits of man mainly, if not only, as sources of wealth, and on the promotion of trade as an end that is well gained over every other good. Such a mind may look on time only as a form of space for the doing of business; on education only as a qualification for gainful employments; on a handsome tree only as the loss or gain upon a balance of the commerical value of its yearly growth, and the yield of the ground as it takes up; on a waterfall only as a power for an overshot wheel; on the discovery of new land only as that of new resources of trade; on a newly reached people only as buyers of our wares; and on a war on a people who have never lifted a hand against us, otherwise than as meddlers with their own laws and towns, as a fine opening up of a trade.[21]

Given that history can be an effective guide to the future, William's book on political and moral economy can still be instructive, thought provoking and even perhaps inspiring. There is much in *Labour and Gold* that has relevance for us today. It should certainly ring alarm bells regarding our obsession with economic growth, a circumstance that defiles the environment and may one day choke the earth. William's concern for the environment and society is also reflected in his dialect poem *The Leane* [22] and anticipates the dangers to the community that greed would have on future generations.

The Leäne

They do zay that a travellèn chap
Have a-put in the newspeäper now,
That the bit o' green ground on the knap
Should be all a-took in vor the plough.
He do fancy 'tis easy to show
That we can be but stunpolls at best,
Vor to leäve a green spot where a flower can grow,
Or a voot-weary walker mid rest.
'Tis hedge-grubbèn, Thomas, an' ledge-grubbèn,
Never a-done
While a sov'rèn mwore's to be won.

The road, he do zay, is so wide
As 'tis wanted vor travellers' wheels,
As if all that did travel did ride,
An' did never get galls on their heels.
He would leäve sich a thin strip o' groun',
That, if a man's veet in his shoes
Wer a-burnèn an' zore, why he coulden zit down
But the wheels would run over his tooes.
Vor 'tis meäke money, Thomas, an' teäke money,
What swold an' bought
Is all that is worthy o' thought.

Years agoo the leäne-zides did bear grass,
Vor to pull wi' the geeses' red bills,
That did hiss at the vo'k that did pass,
Or the bwoys that pick'd up their white quills.
But shortly, if vower or vive

32

Ov our goslèns do creep vrom the agg,
They must mwope in the geärden, mwore dead than alive,
In a coop, or a-tied by the lag.
Vor to catch at land, Thomas, an' snatch at land,
Now is the plan;
Meäke money wherever you can.

The childern wull soon have noo pleäce
Vor to plaÿ in, an' if they do grow,
They wull have a thin musheroom feäce,
Wi' their bodies so sumple as dough.
But a man is a-meäde ov a child,
An' his limbs do grow worksome by plaÿ;
An' if the young child's little body's a-spweil'd,
Why, the man's wull the sooner decaÿ.
But wealth is wo'th now mwore than health is wo'th;
Let it all goo,
If 't 'ull bring but a sov'rèn or two.

Vor to breed the young fox or the heäre,
We can gi'e up whole eäcres o' ground,
But the greens be a-grudg'd, vor to rear
Our young childern up healthy an' sound;
Why, there woon't be a-left the next age
A green spot where their veet can goo free;
An' the gookoo wull soon be committed to cage
Vor a trespass in zomebody's tree.
Vor 'tis lockèn up, Thomas, an' blockèn up,
Stranger or brother,
Men mussen come nigh woone another.

Woone day I went in at a geäte,
Wi' my child, where an echo did sound,
An' the owner come up, an' did reäte
Me as if I would car off his ground.
But his vield an' the grass wer a-let,
An' the damage that he could a-took
Wer at mwost that the while I did open the geäte
I did rub roun' the eye on the hook.
But 'tis drevèn out, Thomas, an' hevèn out.
Trample noo grounds,
Unless you be after the hounds.
Ah! the Squier o' Culver-dell Hall

Wer as diff'rent as light is vrom dark,
Wi' zome vo'k that, as evenèn did vall,
Had a-broke drough long grass in his park;
Vor he went, wi' a smile, vor to meet
Wi' the trespassers while they did pass,
An' he zaid, 'I do fear you'll catch cwold in your veet,
You've a-walk'd drough so much o' my grass.'
His mild words, Thomas, cut 'em like swords, Thomas,
Newly a -whet,
An' went vurder wi' them than a dreat.

In *The Life of William Barnes* William's daughter Lucy reveals that some of his poems had the potential to be politically influential. William would probably have felt uncomfortable if he had been too closely identified with the Diggers,[23] Levellers,[24] Trades Unionists[25] and Chartists,[26] but in my view he holds an honourable place amongst them. Although these movements adopted differing strategies to achieve social and political change they shared a firm belief in the common good. The Diggers were the most radical of these groups, but interestingly there would have been a meeting of minds between the Digger's leader, Gerrard Winstanley (born 1609) and William Barnes in their opposition to enclosures. William would have found no difficulty in giving a positive answer to the final part of the question posed by Gerrard Winstanley in his *The New Law of Righteousness* (1649)....

Was the earth made to preserve a few covetous, proud men to live at ease, and for them to bag and barn up the treasures of the earth from others, that these may beg or starve in a fruitful land; or was it made to preserve all of her children?

In *Labour and Gold* William introduces the spirits *Go-a-head* and *Look-a-head*. *Go-a-head's* task is to reduce all human endeavour to the base motive of profit, irrespective of the harmful effects on the human condition. The wise spirit *Look-a-head's* task is to counsel caution and to bring people to an understanding that it would be a blessing if the common good was considered to be of paramount importance.

William's use of *Go-a-head* is both a rebuke to today's corporate capitalists and a clear indication of William's belief that the economy should be built around the needs of *all* people.

We are still not so free of *Go-a-head* that we cannot learn from William's book on political and moral economy.

Let's hear it for William Barnes.

Ken Griffiths
Fiducia Press
March 2003.

Whitcombe church, two miles south east of Dorchester, where William Barnes preached his first and last sermons.

VIEWS

OF

LABOUR AND GOLD

BY

WILLIAM BARNES, B.D.

London:

JOHN RUSSELL SMITH

36, SOHO SQUARE

1859

PREFACE

KIND READER,

The substance of the following Notes was formed for a Course of Lectures on Labour and Gold. I have now wrought it up into a rather fuller and more exact shape, in which I beg to offer it to your judgement.

Your obedient Servant,

W. BARNES.

LABOUR AND GOLD

LABOUR, GOLD, AND CIVILIZATION

Man is born for action and labour, in the winning of his living in that state of life to which it pleases God to call him. The labour of man in that form of life which we call the *savage* state, is the making of his gear for the winning of his food, whether in hunting, shooting, fishing or seeking the wild fruits of his land, and the making of his clothing and tent or hut; and man's labours in this state are mainly of a kind to perfect the action and form of the body with the senses, and therefore enough, and not too much, for its health. All his muscles are brought into nearly even action by walking and running at all paces, sitting in all forms, by climbing, crouching, swimming, leaping, wielding of weapons, and bearing of weights; and his sight by watching for forms and tokens of animals and fruits; his ear by listening for remote and light sounds; his smelling by the sundry aromata of a fresh land; his mind by induction from sense tokens to the truth of the object of his pursuit.

In Raleigh's expedition to Guiana, Topiowary, king of Aramaia, one hundred and ten years old, walked to and fro fifty-six miles in one day, to see Raleigh. Hala Api Api, a Tonga chief, was, "beyond conception, swift of foot; to see him run you would think he outstripped the wind."

The wonderful boldness and agility of some tribes of Calmucks in the catching of wild horses, and of the Mandan Indians in horse riding, are tokens of some effects of free hunting and nomadic life. Then, again, the wilder tribes of man win great keenness of the senses, with no slight powers of reasoning, in the tracking of animals and men, and the finding of water, and sundry kinds of food. The Pawnees have wonderfully keen sight for the trail of a tribe, and can tell how many they were of men or women, and how many horses they had, how long they halted, and when they went onward. Some Africans told Mr. Burchell, from wheel tracks, that they were those of a waggon that had gone on south-east two years ago; and an Englishman's sagacity in spooring animals comes off with very little honour from a trial against that of the African hunters. The Arabs (*teste* Layard) can tell from the footsteps of a camel whether he was loaded or burdenless, lately fed or hungry, tired or fresh, and ridden by a Bedouin or townsman. Layard was begged not to alight, that his footmarks might not betoken the European, and his deloul was led lest it should be seen it was guided by a novice.

When man begins to till the ground he betakes himself to a new form of life and of toil. Labour is still his lot; but while the work of the community becomes more sundry, that of the individual is likely to become less so, as civilization has a tendency to divide labour, and give to each man work of one particular kind, and thus to make for him a hand and mind of only one skill. Is this a good or evil? Not wholly a good. Indeed, I believe that excessive division of labour is most pernicious to the workman's health and to his perfection as a man.

If a man, in a less refined community, made needles for his household, the grinding of them would happen so seldom, and hold on through so short a time, that it would never break up his health; whereas, with our division of labour, a man takes the grinding of needles as his only work, and breathes steel dust all day, and from day to day, and thus inhales disease and hasty death.

In the work of a waggon-builder or coach-maker, if a man made a whole wheel, the shaving of spokes would come in its turn with other kinds of work that would call the workman into sundry postures, with sundry muscles in action; whereas, when by a more exact division of labour, one man is confined only to the shaving of spokes, he may have a daily onholding pressure on the stomach that may soon affect his health. Thence it is that sundry callings breed their own diseases and deformities; and the glass-blower's life or health is soon spent by constant hot and cold blasts, and thirstings and drinkings; and the miner of mercury is slowly killed with the fumes of quicksilver. "The life of the poor miner himself (in Cornwall as it has been printed) is a short and painful one;" and the overworking sempstress falls pale in early death.

An Iceland farmer may be his own timber and iron worker, and may make his own implements, and build his own house, and weave his own wadmel, and, therefore, may hand less helplessly on others; but an Englishman, with only capital, without handskill, if he loses his capital, which works for him, may have left a pair of hands unskilled, and so quite insufficient for his livelihood.

In the times of the distaff and spindle and spinning wheel, a young woman, while she learnt to spin, learnt also to wash, and sew, and knit, and quilt, and milk, and make cheese, and to cook sundry kinds of food; but if a girl now spends all her days beside a frame or bobbin, waiting only on its winding thread, her hands may become almost useless in a house, and she may be only another machine, a fitting companion only to the frame and bobbin, but ill qualified for the offices of a wife or mother.

But there is a painful, if not loathsome, disease which seems to follow civilization, - caries of the teeth. Pickering, in the Feejee Islands, did not meet with an instance of a rotten tooth, nor did Barnet Burns meet with one among the true uncivilized Maories, and the red men of America were happy with bright and lasting rows of masticators. The jaws of the old Britons, who have been buried in the barrows on Ridgway Hill, contained teeth that were all worn, but yet all sound; and one of the men who were digging out some of the bones of an old seemingly British burial ground on Fordington Hill, when it was lowered, cried out, "They werden a-plagued wi' tootheäche in them days." Pirard de Laval found the natives of the Maldives altogether unacquainted with toothache, but they chewed betel, and were careful of the cleaning of their teeth. The natives of the bay of St. Augustine (*teste* Commodore Beaulieu) had teeth very white, even and small, and rubbed them much with a small piece of wood. But, as a writer says, "nature in its civilized condition is less perfect in the dental process than perhaps in any other;" whether it may be from alcohol, hot drinks, sweets, overfeeding, indigestion, contraction of the jaws, or too little mastication from refined cookery, or from somewhat else. A gold-stuffed tooth has been found in an Egyptian mummy, and the refined Romans often laughed with bad or false teeth, as is shown by Martial.

The natives of the Kingsmill, or Tarawan cluster of islands (Pickering), make a kind of molasses of cocoa palm, and were the only islanders of the Pacific with decayed teeth. The early caries of the teeth in Americans has been imputed to their bolting of their food, and to their sugar and molasses, and hot bread, and hot tea, with iced water. The Tonquinese and Siamese blacken their teeth, as they think it unbecoming to wear them white like cats and dogs.

The laws of health seem to require that while we think and behave as Christian philosophers, we should feed like squirrels, and exercise ourselves like monkeys.

If it were asked whether any form of life could be deemed a good one from which man should find his limbs rotting from his body, what answer could be given to it but "No!" Is such an evil the natural curse of civilization?

CAPITAL

LET us suppose that there are one hundred Robinson Crusoes on an island of fine soil and climate, and food, plants, and animals, with which man's call only for needful life-gear is answered by a uniform but slight daily toil. Let one man have worked 180 hours more than have won his life-gear, and he will have 180 hours or units of life-gear in store. This is *Capital*. He may spend the 180 hours in work for a neighbour who is ill, and live the meanwhile on his 180 units of life-gear, and then his neighbour owes him 180 units of labour or life-gear: it is *Capital*. His neighbour may hand him over 180 bits of metal, gold or silver, each equal in worth to one hour's labour, as each may have taken, on an average, one hour's labour to bring it from the soil into its last form: they are *Capital*.

Capital is accumulated or stored, but transferable, labour or work-store. Labour holden in its own form, or the form of something it has yielded for man's life-gear. Capital is good; yes, but like many other goods, has evils in its train. The sick man needed life-gear in his sickness, and if he had holden capital of his own he would not have needed to borrow it. His capital would have been good. If no other man could have lent or given him life-gear by capital, me may have died. Capital was good to him. If no other man had holden life-gear in store, - capital, - and would still have lent him some, he, the lender, must have worked more hours than those of his own life-gear, to have created capital for the sick man. Capital already stored was good. But it is not a good to the sick man to owe life-gear to the other. It would be a great evil to owe the lender more than he could win over the calls of his own need through the rest of his life; since in that case he would always be owing his neighbour a share of his own body in body's work; and wherever capital alone is fairly yielding life-gear to an unworking man, flesh and blood must be somewhere in the evil plight of owing it to him.

Without question, it is the will of God that man, in his strength, should make capital, as it is His will that a father should find life-gear for his little children, and that, as children become men, they may owe and pay the store of labour lent them by their fathers and mothers in their childhood: but then, again, the accumulation of much capital with fathers will tend to kill a lively piety of thankfulness in their children, and sometimes make them unworksome and vicious spendthrifts. The Hindoos have a tale of a man who bought every day eight loaves, and was asked by a neighbour wherefore he needed so many. He answered:-
(1) Two I keep, (2) Two I give away,

(3) Two I lend, and (4) Two I pay.
He meant (1) He kept two for his own food, (2) Gave two to his mother-in-law, (3) Gave two to his children, and (4) Gave two to his father and mother.

A community without capital or stored labour would be in an evil plight in bad seasons, or times of war or great sickness; and yet the owing of the borrowed capital of the national debt is a fearful call on the working hands of the kingdom.

Some have called what I define as capital by the name of *credit,* and it may be true that lent capital is virtually *credit,* though I do not think it is well called by such a name as is often bestowed on somewhat very unlike it. It is often said that the credit of a man without capital is good, or that he has credit; where credit may mean trustworthiness, or a worthiness of the loan of capital, but not capital itself.

BARTER AND MONEY

BUT no tribe of men would long remain in the state of my imaginary islanders, with each winning every kind of his own body-gear, and no one working out more of one kind of commodity than another of them.

The Britons of Portland, in early times, might have more seafish and less timber or cattle than those of the valley of the Frome, and thence might begin a traffic in which one man or tribe would barter the body-gear of his store for that of another. But after a time again, with the increase of population and of the kinds of body-gear, barter itself would be felt unhandy, as one man or tribe might need some commodity from the store of another who might not want his; and thence would be sought a commodity which would be a measure of labour, and pass for it with all men - Money. Other metals and other bodies besides gold and silver, have been taken for money, as cowry shells among the Hindoos, cacao seeds with the Indians of middle America, and by the Indians of North America, wampum made of clam shell, cut into blocks and ground and polished. The Africans of Loggun are said to have iron money, as Caesar says the Britons had a money of iron rings.

It will be said that money was a noble step in social wealth. Money is a great good. *Yes,* with great evils in its train. That the love of it is the "root of all evil," is a Christian truth which was almost conceived by a heathen - Virgil - when he cried -

"Quid non mortalia pectora cogis
Auri sacra fames!"

O cursed yearning for gold, to what crime dost thou not instigate the hearts of men! It is true that evil minds would be tempted to crime by sundry kinds of life-gear if there were no money; but yet few of them are so handy as money for the thief, the burglar, the robber, the murderer, the forger, and rogue of every kind. A robber would rather kill a man for his money than his carriage and horses, or his tables and chairs, or coats or shoes, since they may be, for him, unhandy forms of goods which could be effectually claimed; but money becomes at the will of the holder anything he may desire; and so, when Mr. Fortune's trunk was one night taken and rifled in China, the thieves kept his money, and then called to his boatman to take back the white devil's goods.

When Mariner explained to Finow, the king of Tonga, the nature and use of money, he no sooner understood the good of it than he perceived the evil of it. He said, "Certainly money was much handier and more convenient; but then, as it would not spoil by being kept, people would store it up instead of sharing it out as a chief ought to do, and thus become selfish; whereas, if provision was the principal property of a man, - and it ought to be, as being both the most useful and the most necessary, - he could not store it up, for it would spoil, and so he would be obliged either to exchange it away for something else useful, or share it out to his neighbours, and inferior chiefs, and dependents, for nothing." He concluded by saying, "I understand now very well what it is that makes the Papalangis so selfish - it is this money." Mariner once complained to Finow that he had been sorely tried by hunger, though the King told him that he only was to blame for it, since, whenever he might see people eating in a house, he was welcome to walk in and share their food; but Patoo Mata Moigna, a Tonga chief, and his wife, went with an English ship to Botany Bay, where he saw people eating in a cook-shop, and thought the good housefather was sharing out food in the Tonga fashion, and went in with the claim of hunger, but was speedily kicked out with the foot of the man who had been born in a land of the Bible.

Mr. Shaw was nearly drowned in fording a river in California, but was helped out and freely fed and sheltered in an Indian's tent; but when, afterwards, he went breadless and almost naked to sleep in a smithy, he was discovered in the morning by a man of his own speech, and sent out, like the Tonga chief at Botany Bay, by a *vis a tergo.*

Among some tribes of an early form of civilization, cattle has been a standard of commercial worth, as an Englishman had learnt that a Kafir bride had cost her bridegroom twenty cows; and our word *fee* is a form of a Teutonic, or Saxon, German, and Danish one - which means cattle; and it has been thought that the Latin *pecunia,* money, is from *pecus,* cattle.

COIN

GOLD and silver are taken for money for several qualities. Gold is a fine metal, very ductile and malleable, so that one grain of it in gold leaf will overspread four hundred square inches, and that 300,000 gold leaves will make only an inch in thickness. Gold is a metal of great tenacity and hardness, so that a golden wire, of one-tenth of an inch thick, will bear a weight of five hundred pounds, and it will waste but slowly in wear. The alchemists said it was harder to destroy gold than to make it. It is a clean metal and oxydizes so slowly from the air as to be almost unrustsome; it can be made, however, to form compounds with oxygen, such as oxide of gold, and peroxide of gold.

Another excellence of gold for money is its scarceness, so that it takes an average of much labour to win a small weight of it. If gold were as readily yielded and as easily won as lead or iron, it would be of as little worth, as rated against lifegear; and a man going to market to buy cattle with ready money would need a cart-load of it; or a lady coming to town for silks, or linen, or groceries, could never, with her own strength, bear her cash.

Before the precious metals were coined, they passed from hand to hand by weight; and so Abraham weighed to Ephron the silver for his land; and the shekel, the talent, the mna and the drachma was a weight, as our pound sterling was at first a pound weight of silver; and our word to expend money is the Latin *expendo,* to weigh out.

Herodotus had understood that the Lydians were the first coiners of gold and silver money, and Crœsus, king of Lydia, carried on gold-diggings in the basin of the basin of the Pactolus, and was so rich that "as rich as Crœsus" means, with us, rolling, as it were, in riches.

There is reason to believe that the silver penny was the first of English silver coins, though the Saxons has a stic or mite of copper. The Saxon penny, like its fellow, the ceiniawg of the Welsh in the tenth century, was, for hundreds of years, the standard coin of the kingdom, though it varied from time to time in size and worth. Many German States own a coin, the *pfenning*, that bears a form of our name *penny*, or the Saxon *peneg*; but the German pfennings, are either of not more, or else of much less, worth than our farthing.

Edward I coined silver *groats*, and Edward III made *half-groats* and gold *florins*. Afterwards came forth gold *nobles*, worth 6s. 8d., and gold *marks* worth 13s. 4d., and these were the coins which were dropped, as fees, by clients into the hands of their lawyers, and which, though they no longer reward the learning of the ready-writer with their glittering presence, have yet marked charges for his offices, his 6s. 8d. and 13s 4d.

Edward IV, in 1465 coined angels, worth 6s. 4d., and half-angels; and Henry VII issued *shillings* in 1504. The name of our *shilling* belongs to a cluster of objects named from the root *skl* to divide off, as in thin lamina; and the noun root *skl* a thin flat substance; and thence we have *scale* of balances, or of a fish, *shell* of a fish or nut, *skull* of the head, *shield, shelter* and *shallow*, and *skilling, shilling*. The Saxon *shilling* was five pennies; a Scotch shilling is one penny. The *skilling* or *schilling* is a coin of Sweden, Norway, Denmark, and Hamburgh, though it is either less or not more than our penny.

Henry VI coined gold ryals, of 10s., and half-ryals and quarter-ryals; and Edward VI gave out the crown, half-crown, sixpence and threepence. Charles II coined guineas in 1663, and in 1672 he sent forth copper half-pence and farthings, which were a welcome supply of small change for tradesmen, who had theretofore felt it needful to strike half-pence and farthings in their own names. The cases of county Museums, and the trays of several collectors, contain many specimens of provincial tradesmen's copper coins. George III issued copper pennies and two-penny pieces.

The *Ducat* is a coin of sundry worth in the south of Europe, from almost as low as half-a-crown to nearly a crown. Coins of sundry states have taken the names or titles of rulers or nobles; as our *Sovereign;* the Portuguese *Re,* king. The old Turkish *Sultanee,* the *Ducat, Ducato,* dukedom, or duke; our *Noble;* the Indian *Ashrufee* (noble); the French *Louis,* the king's name; and the old *Persian Daric.*

Bearing in mind that people so often need to take or pay money in all-but darkness and in great haste, as at the railway counter, I cannot but feel, with Mr. Marsden in his decimal system, that all our sundry coins, whether of the same metal or not, should be of clearly sundry sizes, and of sundry elements of form. I think that *groats* and *florins* are rather a hindrance than help in the reckoning of money. Gilt sixpences have been passed for half-sovereigns, and the groats of a collection, or the takings of a savings' bank, only baffle a man in the making up his pounds.

The Madras fanams are little round flattened dumps, and I think that the rims of silver coin might be bevelled in a circle, like that of the cheese or ovary of the mallow; and then if the gold coins only had milled rims, and copper ones had plain ones, no coin of either of the three metals would be mistaken for another, even in the dark.

CAPITAL AND BULLION

BULLION should not be mistaken for capital. Capital and bullion are different things, as one of them may increase while the other is constant. The bullion of a people is the weight of the money or money-metals under their hands; and the capital of a people is their quantity of stored labour, or of their labour on hand in any form, or in all forms of life-gear.

Suppose that a worksome people may have on hand over their need, at the end of a year, a great quantity of labour stored in sundry forms of life-gear. It is their capital. Then suppose that the next year they do not win by work more life-gear than they consume, but sell some of their stored life-gear for money - then they have more bullion, but not more capital, since they have only increased their bullion by a diminution of their life-gear; and though the bullion is capital, yet it only takes the place of the capital it bought, and sent away from the sellers of it. If the people have not worked at all through the year, they have lessened their capital by their own consumption, and without labour there is no increase of capital.

If a girl, with the run of wide fields, had picked mushrooms worth twenty units of labour, they would be capital. Then if she sold five units of labour in mushrooms for five pieces of silver or gold , her bullion would be increased, but her capital would be the same as it was before her sale of mushrooms; she would have three-quarters of it in mushrooms, and one quarter in specie. So a nation may sell life-gear for gold, and increase their bullion without an increase of their capital; though it may be said with truth, that capital may increase in one land with an increase of gold in another.

A piece of gold, in an ornament or other form, may be offered to the mushroom-picker for mushrooms, and she may not have mushrooms enough for it, and may therefore go out and work harder through the day, or in the evening with a lantern, and so may increase her capital for the sake of the commodity in gold; and so if the yield of gold increases in one land, the men of another may work harder, and make more goods or capital to win it: may rise from a bolted meal, cast their child from their knee, slight the soothing hour of prattle with their wife, and the meditation in the field or bench at eventide, give up the sight of the blue vault of heaven, the cheering sunlight, and the air of the sweet summer field, fall down wholly spent on the late bed, and rise to toil from a feverish dozing, may slight the seeking of higher kinds of knowledge, and purer forms of pleasure, things better than money, and die a wreck in health and happiness. They may become an over-working or overworked nation of money-makers, and yet may be ready to cry to others, "See our prosperity! how rich we are getting!" and their answer might be, "See your degeneracy! how wan, and sickly, and rickety, and deformed you are becoming!"

Though this may be true, it does not follow that a man should loathe labour, or slight that of his good calling; but it would warn us against the giving up of body and soul, with all other good gifts, for the sake of money.

If a whole people went with wild drivings of pickaxe and spade to the digging of silver, and followed only the digging of it, and making of it into silver tools and vessels, they might have each a silver plate, and knife and fork, but where would be the meat and bread for their silver tackle, and their sustenance. The man that is said, in the fable, to have prayed that his touch might turn all things into gold, had too much of a good thing.

CAPITAL, WEALTH, AND INTEREST

I DO not conceive that *capital* is exactly the same as *wealth,* since *wealth* seems to be life-gear, or the elements of life-gear, either wrought or won, or unwrought or unwon by the hand of man - such as the mineral wealth of unworked mines, or a rich harbour of fish by our shores - whereas *capital* is only the wealth of labour.

When gold was at first flowing in rapidly from Australia, an opinion was holden by some that it would lower the rate of interest: *non sequitur.* If on an average of diggers and times, a pound of gold is now brought to hand with less labour than it was formerly won, it will be of less commercial worth as rated against other goods; but an idea that richer mines of gold would lower that rate of interest could only be conceived with a confusion of capital and bullion.

Some time ago, after we had received for years a streaming influx of gold from Australia, our interest of capital was ten per cent. It may be said, "Oh! but bullion was drained very fast out of the kingdom." Well, but before we had any gold from Australia a man could borrow capital at 5 per cent. Then was twice as much gold gone out of England in the three months of the rising of interest as had come in within five gold-yielding years? or had we only half as much gold in England in 1857 as we had in 1852 or even 1856? I think not. Where, and for what, had half our gold gone from our land? It was hardly given away for nothing; and if it had fetched home its worth of life-gear, then our capital was not diminished, since we had received, in forms of life-gear, the labour or capital which we lost in gold.

Interest is the rent of capital, and would rise or fall with a diminution or misuse of capital; but whatever may be the commercial value of gold, the increase of bullion alone would not of need lower or raise the rate of interest. If a man borrows 100 sovereigns, and gives five sovereigns for the loan of them, his interest is one-twentieth of the principal; and if the 100 sovereigns become of greater or less commercial value, so do the five sovereigns rise or fall with them in worth; so that five high-priced sovereigns will pay for the loan of 100 equally high-priced ones, as fairly as five low-priced sovereigns would pay for the loan of 100 equally low-priced ones.

But if a people, with the capital of fifteen months life-gear in store, were to leave off work for twelve months, they would consume twelve-fifteenths of their life-gear, and would have less to lend, and therefore the loan of it would become of higher worth; or if borrowers or owers of capital had been found by lenders or owners to be all roguish consumers and idle wasters of it, and withholders for ever of both capital and rent, then men with even much capital to lend on usury would become less ready lenders of it, and would withhold it against every thing except very high interest or strong security. A great loss of capital, either from foes or idleness, or from a roguish waste of it by spendthrift borrowers, whether they may be over-traders on false capital or men of pleasure, would raise the rate of interest more than the finding of big nuggets of gold.

Interest, in ancient Greece and Rome, was not unusually more than ten or twelve per cent. Twelve per cent. was for a long time the lawful rate of it at Rome; and after the sacking of the city by the Gauls, it rose by a sudden and great increase, from the scarcity of capital; and thirty, forty, or fifty per cent. has been paid or promised for loans on accommodation bills in England. The usury laws of England in 1546, made ten per cent. the lawful rate, which in 1624 was reduced to eight per cent., and under Queen Anne to five per cent. For some time the Romans were forbidden by the Genacian law, as the Israelites were by a higher one, to take usury from each other; but Roman usurers evaded their law by lending money in the names of Latins, or men of other allied tribes. Aristotle, in his politics, disallows the loan of money on usury, and in his Ethics he classes usurers with panders.

REAL AND COMMERICAL VALUE

IN reasoning on labour, money, and prices, we should be careful to distinguish between the real and commercial value, the life-worth and money-worth, of life-gear. The real value or worth of a commodity is one thing, and the commercial value or worth of it is another.

1. The commercial value may be nothing, and the real value great. The real or life-worth of the air which we breathe is so great that we cannot live an hour without it, but it is given us so freely that its commercial or money value mostly is nothing.

2. The real value of a commodity may be the same, while the commercial value may vary with times and places. Water is of the same real value at Dorchester, at Shaftesbury, and at Melbourne in Australia, but at Shaftesbury its commercial price is higher than at Dorchester; at Melbourne 13s. have been given for a hogshead, and at the diggings one sovereign was once offered for a bucketful of water. The real value of coal may be the same at Newcastle and Weymouth, but the commercial worth of it would be less at the pit than hundreds of miles from it.

3. The real value of a thing may be great, but unknown and unfelt, and so the commercial value of it may be nothing. Thistle seeds and leaves of mercurialis, and woodlice and aphides, or at least many weeds and animals, may be of great real life-worth (good) to us, in chains of the world's beings, but as long as we do not know or feel their good or life-worth, we do not hold them at a commercial worth.

Of such things as have no commercial value, it is sometimes said by a kind of speech, which if it were not of thoughtlessness would seem most wicked, that they are of no good. We may kill a butterfly but not a pheasant, as the pheasant is of good but the butterfly is of none; of no good as life-gear, and of no commercial value, though all the butterflies in the world may still be of as much real good as all the pheasants. Most people would own that cows are good, as they are of commercial value. Then is grass good? Yes, for the growth of the good thing, the cow. Is carbonic acid gas, or the foul breath of man and brutes, of good? No. Yes: for the growth of the good thing the grass for the good thing the cow. When we go back from a thing of commercial value, by the chain of successive beings, we come at last to links of unknown or unfelt service to us, and may be too ready to think them of no value.

4. The real value of a commodity may be greater than that of another, while its commercial value is less. Iron is of more real value than gold, and the life-gear of a nation is of more real value than the money that buys it. This truth is shown by the fact that we could thrive better with iron in the form of tools and other kinds of life-gear, though we might be without gold, than we could with gold and not an ounce of iron in any form; and that tribes of Polynesians and others have lived in health and much happiness with life-gear without money, and none could live a year without any kind of life-gear but gold.

In Davis's voyages at Davis Straits the natives were thievish of iron, which they held in great esteem: "when they saw iron they could not forbear stealing of it." In William Cornelison's, and Schooten's, and Le Maire's voyage at the Island without ground, the natives stole the nails in the cabin windows and the bolts upon doors, and drank wine and ran away with the cup. In Oliver Van Noort's voyage, Ladrones men came to the Dutch ship in scores of canoes, crying *Hiero, hiero.* They would whip a sword out of the scabbard , and dive and swim off with it under water. At Virginia, in the voyage of Captains Amadis and Barlow, in 1584, a vessel had been wrecked twenty years before, and the people had made edge tools with the nails and bolts.

To understand the eagerness of these people for iron, look at the stone celts of the early Britons, and other tribes of the stone axe. Among the old Cymro-Britons, iron-working was a liberal art, and a slave became free if he could make himself a smith.

Money is a form of stored labour, and is of no good where there is no labour-won life-gear, or where there is a fulness of freely-given life-gear. In the Gulistan of

Sadi, is a tale of a man who had lost his way in the wilderness, and while he was dying of hunger, with money in his girdle, he found a bag of pearls. "I shall never forget," he cries, "the relish and delight that I felt as I thought it was parched wheat, nor my bitterness and despair when I found it was *only pearls.*"

Herodotus writes of Crœsus, king of Lydia, that he had heaped up a mighty hoard of gold from diggings in the basin of the river Pactolus, and had overcome the Ephesians, the Ionians, and the Æolians; and that when Solon, the philosopher, was at Sardis, Crœsus showed him his treasury, and asked him whom he thought the most fortunate man? He answered, Tellus the Athenian, for that he lived in a free land, had handsome and good children, who had become fathers and mothers of others no less handsome and good than themselves, and had died for his father-land.

Crœsus asked him who was the next in the rank of fortune? Solon answered, Cleobis and Biton, whose mother was a priestess of Juno, and when on a day they found that her chariot oxen were not ready to take her in time to the temple, they took the yoke on themselves, and drew her to her shrine, and that she prayed for them that they might have the best of rewards, and they soon afterwards died in sleep. Crœsus was angry to find his gold rated lower than those forms of good which Solon had set above it; but Solon answered, "No man should be deemed for-tunate till his death, as in the course of many days, months, and years of life, with no two alike, the worst forms of evil may befal him."

A motto of Louis V, of Germany, and our Queen Elizabeth, was, "Take to sea such goods as you can carry off in a wreck; or get such goods for the voyage of life as you can take on with you if your fortune is wrecked:- faith, knowledge, and skill of hand." It behoves us to bear in mind, in these times of mammon-worship, the clear and great difference between the commercial and real value of things. If working men may have but a small store of things of commercial value, they may still have many things of great real worth.

LABOUR THE MEASURE OF COMMERCIAL VALUE

THE measure of the commercial value of things is labour; but by labour I mean the Latin *Labor,*- both the action of the body or mind on the subject, and the reac-tion of the subject on the body or mind; and, therefore, the wear of health or life. It has been shown that it is not barely utility, or the real value of a thing, which makes the commercial value of it. It has been conceived, however, by some, that the commercial value of a thing is grounded upon scarceness. No, not barely upon scarceness. There is in England less weasel flesh than beef, and less badger quarters than quarters of mutton, and yet the commercial value of weasel flesh and badger joints is less than that of beef or mutton. Preserving the truth that it is not even things of greatest utility as life-gear that are of the greatest commercial value, if it be replied that the flesh of weazels and badgers is not life-gear, it may be shown that if the commercial value of any kinds of life-gear varies with their scarcity, or the greater or smaller supply of them, then scarcity itself resolves itself into labour.

It takes the same labour to seed a field whether it bear a light or heavy crop; but more corn for the same labour is conversely less labour for the same corn, which is therefore of less commercial value for less labour. Or if mushrooms are scarcer, it will take a labour of more steps and longer time to gather a bushel of them, and more labour for the same quantity of mushrooms is conversely less mushrooms for the same labour, and the labour varies inversely with the natural supply of them, and measures their commercial value. The commercial value of commodities is rated by labour, under laws of the Allwise, holding on the minds of men, so that commercial commodities check the price of each other by the mutual experiences of workers, sellers, and buyers.

Let it be granted that on an average it takes, at a given place, ten units of labour to win the gold of a sovereign, and the silver of twenty shillings; therefore a sovereign is worth twenty shillings. Then let a richer mine of gold be found, so that on an average it takes only six units of labour to win the gold of a sovereign, and still ten units of labour to yield the silver of twenty shillings; then the same weight of gold will be worth less silver, for the silver digger will not give his ten units of labour in silver for the other's six units of labour in gold, as he would rather dig gold himself; and therefore the commercial value of gold, measured by silver, will sink.

If among the Maories it took sixty units of labour to bring to hand a piece of Koraddee cloth, reckoning every kind of work, -gathering, scraping, and cleaning the fibre, and weaving the cloth, -and twenty units of labour to win a given quantity of fern-root, then the matting is worth three times the root; and if a root gatherer wanted the cloth for his root, the other would rather get so much root himself, and save the difference of labour - forty units; and thus the commercial values of the root and cloth would be checked one by the other.

Suppose a man is mowing, and earns ten units of life-gear or money, for ten hours' work. He breaks the snead of his scythe, but he knows he can go to the wood and cut a stick, and make a new one with ten hours' labour, and so it is worth to him ten units of life-gear or money. Another man offers him a new snead for fifteen units of life-gear or money. No, he will rather make one with ten units of labour, and so the other man's snead is rated to him by his own labour.

Who, it may be asked, can measure labour in all its bearings? and the answer is labour itself. It is rated by checks of labour on all sides. By the social law of the Allwise, a man cannot win any unlimited quantity of another's labour for a given quantity of his own. Every man's labour is rated in the market by the labour that brings, or could bring, all kinds of life-gear against it.

ACTION AND REACTION OF LABOUR

SOME of the Indian jogees are very sparing of bodily action, as an outwearing of life, and practise *hubs-i-dum,* or holding of the breath, on the ground that a man has, from his birth, a set number of respirations to make, and that he will length-en his life by making them sparingly.

It has already been stated that labour is both the action of the body or mind, and the reaction of the work on the body or mind. The *action* of toasting bread with a short fork, or of picking up a red hot pin, may be but slight, but the *reaction* of the heat of the subject or action on the fingers may be not only very disagreeable but pernicious. In the gathering of nuts the action is that of the feet, with the reach-ings and pullings of the hands, and the bendings of the body; and the reaction is, at least, that of the thorns, brambles, and other underwood on the skin and cloth-ing. In painting or mercury-digging there is the action of the body with the work, and the reaction of the white lead or mercury on the health. In grinding of cutlery there is the action of the labour, and the reaction of the steel-dust on the lungs. If the shepherd in the bush in Australia is not worn by too much action, he meets a reaction of loneliness, which may be trying to his mind. In gold digging there may not be the shepherd's reaction of loneliness, but there may be that of the wateriness or heat of the holes, with other hardships. Chimney sweeping is labour of the action of climbing and brushing, and the reaction of soot on the skin, lungs, and nerves. Some indoor businesses are a labour of moderate action, with an undesirable reaction of confinement from open air, and light, and landscape. In some out-door work a man may not meet with the bad reaction of foul air, or gloom, or eye-sores in filth and ugliness, but he may find overaction, and endurance of heat, or cold, or wet. Standing guard is labour of little action, but is sometimes of bad reaction of cold on the body, and irksomeness on the mind. Marching or drill may be action enough for heat and lung-health, with a bad reaction of compulsory con-tinuance at the will of another. The action of the calling of a foot-soldier in bar-racks is not overmuch, and yet it seems from the statistics of life in the army, that the reaction of it is most deadly, killing the soldier at half of his fair length of life. In some great quarries or mines one may find a population with a saddening share of mis-shapen people and cripples and idiots, and hear of many deaths and muti-lations from fire-damp and choke-damp in coal mines; and of every five men employed in the taking of the edible birds' nests (*teste* Osborns' Quedah), two are killed in their work, whence the nests are of very high price. The life of the Cornish miners is a sad and short one; and the most trying operations in the cot-ton mill are willowing, batting, and carding; the rooms in which they are carried on are clouded with fine particles of cotton, which sometimes set a stranger cough-ing; most of the men in these rooms (as a writer saw them) "were pallid in their complexions." Glass blowers work in heat from 70 degrees to 100 degrees; many of them are bathed in perspiration from heat (the *reaction*) only, for their labour (*action*) is very moderate. They get coughs and colds, and find their labour weak-ening work. Some of them drink to slake their thirst two gallons of beer a day; and though it may be found a kind of present help, it is not taken without a bad reaction on the stomach.

When a man feels the especial evil of the action or reaction of his own calling, he is ready to wish he had his neighbour's instead of it; while his neighbour may be longing for that of a third man as far better than that in which he plies his hands or mind. While we observe that some kinds of labour may have a painful reaction on the mind, we ought not to overlook those which may have a bad reaction on the conscience; and which, however easy may be their action, and however great may be their gain, are not to be earnestly chosen by Christian men; since, as they dead-en the conscience, they likewise do harm to the soul.

The keeping of a gambling-house, or a house of ill-fame, the buying and selling of stolen goods, the adulteration of food and drink, and businesses in which great gain may be made by lying, and the deceiving of unwary people. The office of common hangman, and the work of the slave trade, from that of the kidnapper or slave maker, to that of the taskman, are instances of kinds of labour, which, however good in its kind may be their action, will always bring a pernicious reaction on the conscience, and so on the soul.

EXCHANGE, &c.

VARIATION of exchange arises from the increase or decrease of bullion, and not of capital, whereas variation of interest arises from increase or decrease of capital, and not of bullion.

If a people, A, of one land sell for gold to a people, B, of another land, more life-gear than they take of them, a balance of gold should flow from B to A, and gold will become of greater value with B by the labour (or cost) of transmitting it to A; and so it happens that in the commerce of two peoples, gold may be sometimes of higher worth with one, and at other times with the other, or that the exchange is against one or the other; and the rate of exchange is deemed to be against the people with whom the gold is of higher worth, as it will sink in value by transmission, for life-gear, to the other people.

For the sake, therefore, of a people's money, it is deemed needful that they should sell to another people as great worth of life-gear as they buy of them; but this seemingly harmless truth may have become, in our dealings with China, an evil and a great sin, since the Chinese have, from their own lands and hands, most of the kinds of life-gear that we could sell them from England, and so we push upon them the sale of a poison - opium.

Commodities brought by labour from their source are of higher commercial value by the labour that brings them to their place of sale, and thence the loss of selling goods up the stream of their transmission, or, as we say, of carrying coals to Newcastle.

The mint price of standard gold is £3. 17s. 10 1/2 d. per ounce, but as the commercial value of specie would vary by the balance of trade or rate of exchange, so the commercial value of gold in the lump, against sovereigns or other gold coins, in a land of gold mines, as in Australia, would vary by the labour which brings the sovereigns to hand, or by the balance of labour of keeping, weighing, reckoning, and paying gold in the lump, and of keeping and paying sovereigns. But no variation of the value of gold against sovereigns in Australia can be a measure of the variation of the commercial value of gold, as rated against other kinds of life-gear, since one cannot find the variation of the commercial value of a commodity by rating it against itself, any more than one can find the motion of a ship by taking the distance from her binnacle to her bow.

A quart of milk will still be worth a quart of the same milk, and a pound of flour a pound of the same flour, whether the commercial value of milk or flour be rising or falling; and it would not be good reasoning to conclude that silver has not risen or fallen in commercial value since this time last year, because both yesterday and yesterday twelve-months I got three silver groats for a shilling; for an ounce of silver will be worth an ounce of silver as constantly as a quarter of wheat is worth eight bushels of it.

Gold and silver are under the same law of labour and commercial value as other commodities, though some may overlook this truth; and since there is a kind of legal standard of the value of gold as rated against the sovereign, which is made of alloyed gold, with a constant quantity of labour, they may think that money differs from all other commodities in a freedom from the laws of labour to which they yield; and that while their commercial value is daily shifting, that of money will continue steadfast.

It would be as idle to pass a law that a pound of gold should be always equal to the same quantity of labour, either in kind or in life-gear, as it would be to try to fix the planets in space. An ounce of gold, with some allowances for the alloy of sovereigns and the labour of the coining them, will be of nearly the worth of the sovereigns it will make; though a sovereign may be worth a little more or less of raw gold in Australia at one time than another, from the scarceness or manifoldness of sovereigns, as well as from the labour of their freight from England, and their handiness over that of gold-dust or nuggets for the office of money.

COMPOUND LABOUR

AN objection may be cast by many against the truth that labour is the measure of commercial value, inasmuch as sundry men - diggers, craftsmen, and professional men - are paid unequally for the same quantity of labour, whether it may be measured by action or time; and thence one should observe the difference between simple and compound labour.

The picking of mushrooms, where the picker has the free run of the fields, is what may be called simple labour, since the basket is of so small a worth that it may be left out of calculation. But the commercial value of a pound of truffles is greater than that of a pound of mushrooms, even if the truffle hunter can gather a pound of truffles with as little action as that which wins a pound of mushrooms, since truffle hunting is a compound labour. The truffle hunter needs a truffle dog, and (1) his truffle dog does not come to hand without labour in the training of him, and (2) the dog must have food, which is the labour that brings it to hand. (3) He needs a spade or some other tool, which is also labour; and, therefore, the pound of truffles comes to hand only by the labour of the hunter, and three or four other quantities of labour, on which it takes its commercial value.

So also hand-skill and mind-skill are cases of compound labour. The craftsman's work takes up his own labour, with a share of the labour spent in the form of his premium, and in his life-gear and tools, and in the labour of his own hands and mind in the learning of his craft.

So also the physician's labour is that of his own action of mind and body, with the labour spent in the form of money for his schooling and training, and his premium and life-gear while he was working for his skill; his own former mind-labour of many years, the labour which brings to hand his needful books, and his needful carriage or horse, and even a share of the labour of former minds in the advancement of the science of physic. Thence the prophets and apostles were not allowed to take fees for their healings, or to sell their freely-bestowed powers of the Holy Ghost. Freely they had received, freely they were to give. Whereas our physicians earn most of their skill by labour, and may give it for the labour of others.

So in the fine arts. The picture of a great painter may win a great price, which is grounded on its excellence, and that on the labour spent on the painting of it, and on a great deal of other labour, such as the labour of his life-gear for his years of study - that of a premium or of fees to masters - that of years of unpaid or underpaid toil to win his handskill, and that of the time spent in watching nature in man, in brutes, or in the landscape; in rocks, water, trees, and flowers; in feeling, action, form, and colour; and of all that meet the eyes of man in God's world. In short, it often happens that so many of the earlier years of the worker for the minds of men are so ill paid that he dies almost breadless before he attains well-paid fame; or else, as a homely saying speaks, he cannot win bread till he has no teeth left to eat it. Yet it may be true that a work of fine art for the mind of man may not be always so truly rated by labour or transference as work for bodily life-gear. A great man's work is that of his own soul's thought, his own feeling, his own hand, his own skill, and no other man can give its like.

VARIATION OF PRICES

WE say of the variations in the money prices of commodities, that they are rising or falling, and often talk as if money always remained of the same commercial value, while that of other commodities was shifting, whereas specie, like all other products of labour, takes its value from the labour spent on it.

Let the compound labour which shall have brought an acre of wheat to hand be eight hundred units. One year let the acre yield twice as much as it yielded in the former year; then in the latter year, as the same labour yields twice the quantity of wheat, so conversely the same wheat is yielded by half the quantity of labour, and becomes of less commercial value. So let a pound of gold be brought to hand on an average of five years, by four hundred units of labour, and then let so gold-bearing a soil be found that on an average of the next five years, the same four hundred units of labour will yield two pounds of gold, and as the same labour yields twice the gold, so conversely the same gold is yielded by half the labour, and it becomes of less commercial value.

To us, on the ongoing earth, it looks as if the earth were still and the sun were moving; and to a child who may be riding by a row of trees between him and the moon, the moon would seem to be going on beside him; and when it seems to us that the prices of commodities are rising or falling, the truth may be that gold is becoming of less or greater commercial value, while the labour value of the commodities is steady. If commodities are not won, while gold is brought to hand, with less or more labour than they were a hundred years ago, then their greater or less money-worth is owing to the less or greater commercial value of gold or silver as money metals.

A man may be told, with truth, that he may earn twice as much gold for a week's work in some other land as he can in England; but he may not be told, what may be likewise true, that his life-gear would take in that land twice as much gold as it would cost in England. A coat which might be bought for three pounds in England, would at one time have cost nine pounds in Australia; so that with wages of threefold their English measure in gold, the coat would cost as much, and only as much, labour in Australia as in England. Upon collecting the prices of sundry kinds of life-gear in Australia, at the stirring times of the early diggings of gold, I find that the sum of them was manifold of that of the prices of the like life-gear with us at home.

If, in the olden time, when a man earned a silver penny for a day's work in England, it would buy the life-gear of twenty-four such weights of silver with us, then silver was of twenty-four times its present commercial value, and his six pennies a week were as high wages as would now be twelve of his shillings.

A four years' diary of a landowner and farmer of his estate in Dorset, a little more than one hundred and fifty years ago, gives the prices of labour and of the sundry kinds of life-gear that was consumed at that time in the household of a squire, and shows that one pound weight of his gold or silver was worth three times as much labour or life-gear as is a pound of ours.

TRANSFERENCE OF RATING OF COMMODITIES

THE commercial value of a commodity is not always determined by the labour that may have brought it to hand, as its price is checked by transference of rating to the labour that would yield its like from other hands or minds. (1) There may be a transference of rating from the labour which may have brought a commodity to hand, to that which would bring its equal to hand. Suppose a mower wants a snead for his scythe, and can have a good stick for the cutting of it, and that he or his brother can bring it to his hand with six hundred units of labour; and that another man offers him its equal, which he has brought to hand, for a thousand units of labour; he would not be likely to take it at the seller's price of a thousand units of labour, since he can have one with six hundred units of labour, so that, in his mind, it is to be rated, not by the labour of the workman that has brought it to hand, but by the labour that would bring to hand its equal. (2) There is a transference of rating from the labour which brought a commodity to hand, to the labour which it would take off the hands of the buyer. If I have a work which I can do with four thousand units of labour as I now work on it, and know that with another contrivance of action I can do it with two thousand units of labour, while the contrivance itself will consume only a thousand units of labour, I take the contrivance and save a thousand units of labour by it. Whereas, if the contrivance would cost three thousand units of labour, I should not take it, as it would bring me a loss of a thousand units of labour.

So the buyer of tools and machinery will rate them by the labour they will save, while the maker of them must rate them by the labour that brought them to hand; and that there should be a good and unlosing sale of a tool or machine, it is needful that all the labour it takes off the workman's hands should be greater, or not less, than that which brought it to hand; and thence the absurdity of a most complex machine for drawing a cork, such as that which is shown by Hogarth in one of his pictures, or of a great wheel to break a fly.

From the first case of transference we see why the works of very skilful hands or minds, as paintings of great masters, rise in commercial value upon their death. If a man had a fifty-pound work of a good painter, and asked me one hundred pounds for it, while the painter was alive and ready to make me a riplico of it for fifty pounds, I should most likely not rate the picture higher than fifty pounds, which is the measure of labour that would make me its equal. Then if the painter die, I cannot transfer my rating from the labour that yielded the picture to the labour that would make me its like. The is no such labour. It is lost from the world, and the commercial value of the picture is no longer checked by it. Can it be checked by any thing else? Yes, it can be checked less straitly by sundry ones, and especially by two. (3) By the worth of its reaction on the mind, and (4) there is another transference of rating from the labour which may have brought a commodity to hand, to that which would bring to hand another, which, though it might not be its equal, would be next to it in good service. If I cannot transfer my rating of the best work of the best painter to the labour of its like from the same painter, since he is dead, yet I can feel that the best work of the next best painter is of nearly as fine a service as its own to the mind, and can resolve to give rather less for a rather less excellent picture, and so rate the higher picture by transference of rating from itself to the labour that will yield me, if not its equal, yet its nearly equal in good service to my mind. Thence, although after the death of mighty workmen the commercial value of their works does rise by wild flights, inasmuch as their likes cannot be brought to hand by any labour on the earth, yet it is not infinite, but is checked by the labour of the next excellence in work.

There is another transference of rating from the labour that brings a commodity to hand to the welcome reaction of it. A man who might be dying of thirst on a road, which, owing to some restraint, he could not leave, might be willing to give a sixpence for a glass of water from a spring only fifty steps from him; and Esau gave his birthright for a meal of pottage, rating it as the water would be rated, not by the labour that brought it to hand, but by its welcome reaction on the spent life of the body.

The commercial value of commodities chosen for their good or pleasing reaction on the mind, such as works of the fine arts, and jewellery, and other ornaments, may be rated by the buyer on the worth of their reaction on the mind, as when a man well-tired walks another mile for the sight of a charming landscape, or building, or picture, rating the pleasure of the reaction on his mind against the labour he spends to win it.

Akin to this wholesome reaction of the beautiful, is the less wholesome reaction of the rare, as the glory of having the greatest diamond in the world, or the finest or only robe of a particular kind, or the finest rose or tulip in a land, such as that which was sought among the Dutch in the time of the tulip eagerness; or that of having the only known copy of an old book in bibliomania; or that of the winner in a game of skill or competition for bare excellence of deed or quality.

Thence, again, we see why the slight labours of sycophants in the praising or following of the rich, only as such, and in servile subserviency to the bestowers of moneyworth favours, and in toadihood to the great, are not unfrequently so highly paid in money. These may be rated, not by their own quantity, but by their pleasing services to the mind, the glory, the pride, the arrogance, or the self-love of the rewarders of them.

SUPPLY AND DEMAND

IT appears, then, that labour is the measure of commercial value in several ways: 1st - as the labour which brings a commodity to hand; 2nd - as the labour that would bring its equal to hand; 3rd - as the labour which would bring to hand the commodity next to it in good service; 4th - as the labour for which circumstances call on the buyer without it. It may be answered that it is supply and demand that are the measures of commercial prices. It is not true that supply singly, or demand singly, is a measure of commercial value; as there is a greater supply of mutton than there is of otter flesh, and yet mutton is of the higher price. "Ah! but there is no demand for otter flesh," it may be answered, "it is the demand that gives commercial value." Not singly. There is as great a demand for water as for brandy or eau-de-Cologne, and yet water is of less commercial value than either of those commodities. "Ah!" one may reply, "but it is supply and demand together that measures commercial price." It is labour, for supply and demand can be resolved into labour. The supply of a commodity is the measure of the labour by which commodities are brought to hand; and demand for a commodity is the measure of the labour for which circumstances call on the buyer without it.

If with a natural scarceness or short supply, as of a crop, mushrooms are fewer one season than another, then one takes more steps and spends more time to win a bushel of them, and more labour for the same quantity gives a higher price; but in the case of a greater supply of labour-wrought commodities, as that of over production or a glutted market, the commercial value of them is set by the fourth case of transference, the transference of rating from the labour that brought them to hand, to the labour that the buyer without them is bound by circumstances to give for their service; so that the measure of their value with the demander is as much a measure of labour as is that of the supplier.

If a scythe-snead be offered to a tailor or fisherman, as such, then, since a scythe-snead is not a commodity for which he may be bound by circumstances to give labour, it may be of no worth. If it be offered to a mower without a scythe at the latter end of May, a little before mowing time, then, since it is a commodity for which he is called by circumstances to give labour, it is worth labour to him, but still it is worth only the labour with which he could make out of a good snead-stick in his hands another snead, better, or not worse, than the one offered to him. And now again we see that, if the fisherman were to buy the snead to sell to the mower, or to burn on his own hearth, he would overpay for it with any price greater than that which would bring a snead of as good service to the mower's hands, or a stick of as good service to his own fire. Demand for commodities, therefore, is only the labour which men are bound by circumstances to give for their services, in other commodities of the same or other names.

If Dutch foot-stoves be taken to the West Indies, then, inasmuch as the people are not called by circumstances to give much labour for the keeping of their feet warm, the stoves are of but little worth among them; and if the people at Adelaide had each of them a store of shoes for three years' wear, and yet a cargo of shoes were shipped to them, they would make a case of a glutted market, and would be of little commercial value by the 4th case of transference of rating, since none of the people would be as yet called by circumstances to give labour for shoes; and oversupply or overproduction of commodities brings down their commercial value by a measure of labour of the 4th case of transference of rating.

TRUE WEALTH

TRUE wealth is the happy use of a fulness of happily won or received life-gear. It is not money as such; and a pound weight of specie in one land, owing to a lower commercial value of gold or silver, may not bring more than a half, or a third, of the life-gear which it commands in another.

In the time of the earlier gold-diggings and nugget-findings in Australia, in 1852, I collected the prices in Australia and England of sundry kinds of life-gear, such as food, water, clothing, housing, heating and lighting, hardware, earthenware, house-labour, horse-work, and horses and conveyances, with grooming and fodder, and water conveyance; and at that time, at Melbourne, a sufficiency of all these kinds of life-gear would cost, collectively, nearly five times as much specie as would buy them in England; so that a man earning five guineas a week there would be only as wealthy as an earner of a guinea a week in England; and a writer of a letter in the "Times" spoke of some friends of his who had three hundred a year and could hardly live, as, indeed, we may believe, since their income would yield them the life-gear of only sixty pounds at home; and, notwithstanding, another letter says, "Talk of gold, we are almost smothered in it here," there was then at Melbourne a handsome two-storied pawnbroker's establishment; and a man who advertised for a light porter, received one hundred and fifty answers to his call.

We can readily believe that Melbourne is now in a better state of wealth, since a greater share of the labour of the land is spent in the winning of true life-gear, and less of it to that of the hard metal, which is by itself no life-gear, and which can win it only from the labourers for life-gear. It does not follow that we may have any more wealth from the gold of Australia, since, although we should reckon gold as life-gear, yet the winning of it may have drawn off hands from the winning of life-gear of other kinds.

If in an island, as, for instance, in Pitcairn Island, the people were all working for life-gear, and suddenly one-fifth of them left their winning of food for the winning of fossils, it is clear enough that with an increase of fossils they would find a decrease of life-gear, unless, indeed, the four-fifths should increase their labour by one fourth, which, if they had theretofore done that fair work of their bodily strength, would be a physical evil. If, however, the one-fifth that began to dig for fossils, had theretofore been wholly inactive, then their labours would make the community richer by their fossils, and so no community can be the more wealthy by the digging of gold, unless it is dug by hands hitherto unworking, or unless the finding of it stirs working hands to greater labour. Spain is none the more wealthy for the silver and gold she drew from America, and the wealth of England in all kinds of life-gear and handywork might be no less with less bullion than is the store we now hold.

The Manchester and Salford water company have allowed a hogshead of water a day to a head, but water was at one time 3s. a hogshead at Melbourne, so that the Manchester allowance of water would have cost a guinea a week. If the Israelites had found a gold-yielding creek in the wilderness, and a thousand of them had left the picking of manna for the digging of it, they would most likely have starved; and more welcome to Robinson Crusoe would have been potatoes than nuggets of gold only a spit deep.

It is true that men may win in Australia a fulness of good life-gear and the elements of true wealth and happiness, if they seek them, rather than worse elements of wealth and vicious pleasure; but it was not fair or good that newspapers often mis-led so many working men by stating Australian wages in weight of gold, without the truth of its commercial value. The question for a working man migrating to another town or another land, is not what weight of gold, but what life-gear his week's work will win him. Labour in England may earn more gold than in Switzerland, and yet we may have among us as great a share of half-starved bod-ies as have the Swiss; and we may have as great a share of underfed bodies as could have been found by Captain Cook in the Tonga Islands, where there was no money.

There are three divine gifts which are the elements of true happiness or wealth: the spiritual one of righteousness; the bodily one of health; and the social one of good government; but the more common kinds of worldly wealth are of uncertain effect, though the peace of a community is none the safer for a greater inequality of wealth, such that one class may be over-rich to wanton luxury, while another are poor to naked hunger. It is desirable that every man in health should find he can win the needful life-gear of his climate and life, savage or civilized, by such a quantity of labour as befits his body and mind.

REACTION OF WEALTH

THE good reaction of wealth on the mind is the begetting of thankfulness and beneficence, and happily, through grace, many are the cases in which such is its effect; but still we can hardly help learning by the Bible, and by observation if not experience, that its reaction may be evil. More than one poor soul may have said, "Oh! if I were rich what good would I do!" We have, however, but slight grounds for promising that we should do all good with suddenly-received riches, since new wealth and new power would bring new feelings with new yearnings, each the effect of a new commodity of wealth, and whether our newly-awakened yearnings would be good or evil, spiritual or sensual, for noble or grovelling aims, would arise from our fulness or lack of the better gifts of grace.

The reaction of sudden riches on a mind unhallowed and untrained for the stewardship of them is in many cases most pernicious. It is a saying that it is easier to bear hardship than affluence, though few of us would readily choose the easier task. Many men who have become suddenly rich by the wills of rich kinsmen, or by the chances of a stroke in traffic, or a lottery, or a nugget, have thrown aside the tools of their calling, and having twenty-four hours every day on their hands without any healthy mind-work, either in pursuits of their own, or in offices for the good of others, they have taken up the lowest pleasures that would lead them with agreeable excitement through their empty time.

We have heard of lucky gold diggers who have stifled the reaction of idleness or inaction between buckets of grog, or in the mad pride of the ownership of gold, have washed their feet in a tub of brandy and then thrown it away, and a letter of the time from Australia says "the diggers seldom make less than from £40. to £60. per week, but I am sorry to say that two-thirds of them are doing themselves harm both in body and soul; there are, however, some, although a smaller proportion, who take care of their earnings." Another letter tells us that "some of the diggers make a very bad use of their gold. They think nothing of putting £50. in a landlord's hands, and bide there till it is all spent."

What ground of complaint could a mind that would so spend riches, ever make that the Allwise kept him to a bare sufficiency in a life of toil. Whether the low state of Spain may or may not be the bad reaction of the silver and gold and lands of South America, it is true that her well-being is not upholden by her gain in America. It is said that the area of Spain is twice that of Great Britain, and yet she has a population of only ten millions, and that even of them a large share are wretched. If we would be preserved from such a sad reaction from the gold or other wealth of our colonies, let us be careful to keep them free of slave labour, and ourselves under grace.

One bad reaction of wealth upon some minds may be arrogance or purse pride, with which a man is significantly called by the Persians *mawlmust* or wealth-tipsy; and another of its effects may be a peaceless care against the loss of it, and a dread of some evil chance by which it may be taken away. It is said of Anacreon that he once received from King Polycrates a gift of a talent of gold, but that he sent it back, as he was none the happier for a gift that compelled him to keep on the watch. Juvenal sings:-

"Cantabit vacuus coram latrone viator."

"A traveller with nothing to lose,
Before robbers wont shake in his shoes."

And Lucillius cries:-
"To richer houses, thieves, direct your feet,
Here poverty, the best of guards, you'll meet."

And it might have been against this reaction that the Cynics thought that the gatherings of gold, or of any but the most needful life-gear, was a folly of the worst kind.

Another reaction of wealth may be greediness and the hoarding mind of the miser. The fact that success of labour will make a man more worksome has been given in a homely saying that "when a man finds the world coming, he pulls the harder," and a persevering industry of this kind, while its aim is a fair provision for a man's own house, is not forbidden by the Gospel; but it seems as if it were nothing less than the whole world for which the true miser pulls. Some Englishmen, such as Elwes and Wood, have realized the sketch given of a miser in a Hindoo tale, which is, that a miser was halfway from his house to the mosque, when he recollected that he had left his lamp burning, and went home and called to his boy, "Put out the lamp, but do not open the door, or you will wear the hinge." The boy cried, "Oh! sir, don't you wear out your shoes by coming back so far?" "No," replied his lord, "don't you know that I walked back bare-footed, with my shoes under my arms?"

Another feeling allied to that of miserliness is the money-making mind, which looks on the works of God or the pursuits of man mainly, if not only, as sources of wealth, and on the promotion of trade as an end that is well gained over every other good. Such a mind may look on time only as a form of space for the doing of business; on education only as a qualification for gainful employments; on a handsome tree only as the loss or gain upon a balance of the commercial value of its yearly growth, and the yield of the ground it takes up; on a waterfall only as a power for an overshot wheel; on the discovery of a new land only as that of new resources of trade; on a newly reached people only as buyers of our wares; and on a war on a people who have never lifted a hand against us, otherwise than as meddlers with their own laws and towns, as a fine opening up of a trade.

A writer who, as I understand him, wished to show that the sugar and rum trade of the West Indies could not thrive with free labour, inasmuch as it could not compete with that of slaves, has stated, seemingly without any misgivings of conscience, that he himself had worked slaves eighteen hours a day at cropping time; and the mind with which a writer from Canton seems to weigh even the life of men as nothing against the gain of trade is shocking. He says, in writing of the Chinese who were killed by us in our quarrel with Yeh:-
"At a guess, and nothing more, except judging by the number of dead bodies I have seen, I should say the Chinese lost about a thousand killed during the bombardment and attack. If this loss of life is weighed against the increased prosperity that will, without doubt, be seen and felt in the city after a short period of the rule of the Western Powers, I think the most prejudiced must admit that the course taken has been the most humane." What is his major proposition from which he draws his conclusion? I cannot fancy any but this:- if we can improve the prosperity of a town by shooting a share of its inhabitants, it is humane to shoot them. A proposition with which we should go and shoot every inmate of every unionhouse, and every helpless wretch who is a burden to labour. But where is a Christian to find the matter of such a proposition?

THE WEALTH OF THE CYNIC
PHILOSOPHERS AND THE SPARTANS

IT was against the bad reaction of wealth that the Cynics by their rules, and Lycurgus by his laws, outcast all but the most needful forms of life-gear; and

70

though it may be deemed by most of us in England that they chose a narrowness of living that was below the happy mean of worldly wealth, and foolishly slighted many good rewards of man's toil, yet it must be owned by Christians that their opinions of the evil reaction of money are confirmed by the Gospel, and that little more than food and raiment is proposed by our religion as worthy of our careful yearning.

One of the few utensils retained by Diogenes was a water cup, which, however, on seeing a boy dip water with the hollow of his hand, he threw away as needless; and when, as he was basking in the sun, Alexander stood before him in his sunshine, and asked him what service he should do for him, his answer was, "Why, get out of my sunshine, you are depriving me of more than you can bestow."

The aim of the Lycurgus was to make his people hardy, toilsome, free, and brave, and therefore he formed his laws against luxury, idleness, the love of money, and the fear of death; and besides what is told us of his laws by Greek and Latin writers, we find scattered in their works tales and facts that show us that his code had at length wrought much of his design.

The first, if not the main dish on the Spartan board, was a food which the Latins called *black broth,* and the Spartans themselves *haimatia,* or "blood food," though it is not certain whether it was so called from its colour, or whether it contained any such ingredient as the main one of our black-pudding. It may be believed that it was no great luxury, though the Spartans are said to have relished it. Dionysius, when he once dined at a Spartan table, did not like it, which the Spartan cook could not think wonderful, as it lacked its true sauce, the hunger of toil; and the laws of Lycurgus enacted that people should dine in public, as before their houses or in open-sided rooms, lest the luxury of dainties should find a place at their table.

Another Spartan law was, that youth should not spend their time in idleness in the towns, but should be sent to work on the lands; and they were forbidden to sleep on a soft bed, or to pamper their taste with sauces. This training is not unlike what Captain Spencer gives as that of the young Circassian. He says:- "After the first few years of helpless infancy have passed over, he is taken from his mother, and consigned to the care of some warrior, famous for his skill in the military exercises of his country, who now performs to the young mountaineer the duties of a parent, bearing the title of *Attalick,* and during the whole time the youth remains under the superintendence of his teacher, he is never permitted to visit his parents, lest he should be spoiled by indulgence, or enervated by excessive affection."

To a man who asked Agesilaus what the laws of Lycurgus had done for Sparta, he answered, they had taught them to despise luxury; though, as Lucian "de Saltatione" writes, they had been, or were fond of dancing, and performed to a pipe a dance of many figures, imitative of war, love, and wine. Lycurgus took away the use of gold and silver, as the seeds of all crimes, forbidding goods to be bought for money, but ordaining a trade of barter; and he made an equal division of the lands, as a safeguard against the tyranny of riches; he directed that honours should be bestowed on the old for their years, but he granted none to the rich for their wealth. And he forbad that women should have any dowry, so that wives might be chosen for themselves and not for their money.

"Mulieres pro dotibus potiùs quàm a probitate et formâ seligi, causa non parvi mali evenit. Haud dubitandum est Deum benevolum, uxores ab amore, aut a sensu egregiæ earum vel formæ vel indolis, eligi velle. Ne, a matribus pravis indignè propter dotes ductis, proles pravæ continuò nascantur, donec, vitis cujusque generis, in homines transmissis, gens tota, ne dicam genus totum hominum, vitietur."

The love of money undermines probity and freedom, as it breeds a subserviency in vice, and a readiness to sell the good of one's fatherland for gain. Men may be found who for gold would strengthen the hands of their foes in a war, and nations may be willing to cringe under another from whom they receive great gain or trade, while they would drive a tribe of savages from their lands; and so Parmenion, the Spartan, cries, "I scorn wealth, the nurse of flatterers, nor will I be a slave to a frown (eyebrow). I know the freedom of a homely meal."

The bravery of the Spartans is often the theme of Greek and Latin pens, one of which writes:- "A Lacon being asked why Sparta was not walled, said 'It *is* walled by the valour of its inhabitants.'" And when Xerxes, on his invasion of Greece, wrote to Leonidas, the King of Sparta, "Give up your arms," his answer was, "Come and take them." Leonidas being told that the very sunlight was darkened by the arrows of the Persians, answered, "Oh! it will be nice to fight in the shade;" and when some one told him, "The foes are near us," he answered, "Oh! then we are near them."

The Spartans were forbidden to flee in war, and so an epitaph or epigram on the

Spartans who fell at Thermopylæ, says:-

"O stranger, to the Spartans tell
We kept their laws, and here we fell."

When some one was laughing at a lame Spartan for his folly of going to the war a cripple, he replied "Oh! I don't go to the war to run away, I mean to stand my ground." And the reckless up-giving of life for the freedom of the land was at length strong even in the Spartan women. A mother, on giving to her son the shield of her husband, said to him, "Come home either *with* this shield or *on* it," that is, don't lose it to the foe; rather die and let it be your bier. And another Spartan mother said to a son who came home from the wars lame from a wound, "Never mind, my boy, you will be put in mind of your valour at every step." A Greek epigram makes a Spartan mother to have slain her own son on his fleeing in a battle. "I shall be called an unhappy mother," she cries, "but then it will be in a free land."

The glory of Spartan bravery was the defence of Greece by a few hundred men under Leonidas, against the mighty army of Xerxes, King of Persia, at the pass of Thermopylæ.

The Spartans, who were also called *Lacones,* were not given to waste words in useless talk, whence we have the expression of a *Laconic* answer; nor did they hold in high esteem any useless attainments. A man who had learnt to stand a long time on one leg, said to a Spartan that he did not think any Spartan was a match for him. "May be not," was the reply, "but a goose would beat you."

Unhappily for the institutions of Lycurgus, Epitadeus, when he was one of the Ephori, passed a law that allowed men to alienate their lands, so that the little freeholds began to be gathered into few hands, and most of the people became hirelings; and Agis, a Spartan worthy of his name, withstood the monopoly of the land with no better success than the loss of his life.

There were two evils in the state scheme of the Spartan mind. They aimed at the conquest of other lands, and therefore at the winning of state wealth, and they held slaves, and so disdained some useful kinds of handy-work, and at last they fell.

MONOPOLY AND TYRANNY OF CAPITAL

AT one time a nation may have felt the tyranny of the sworded conqueror, with his martial law or despotic rule; at another, the tyranny of the serf-holding lord, and with a commercial people like the English, labour will be more or less exposed to the tyranny of great working capital. To hold that there is a tyranny of capital is not to hold that every holder of capital is a tyrant, and since the imputation of tyranny may be deemed an imputation of a kind of unrighteousness, it may be right to show the form of that of capital. Tyranny, as it is distinct from lawful kingship, was understood by the Greeks to be the government of the power-winning sword, rather than the lawfully-wielded sceptre; but among us tyranny more often means unrighteously-wielded power, whether it may be holden lawfully or from the sword. By tyranny, as the word is applied to capital, however, I mean that power by which it lessens men's full freedom in the doing of fair acts which are lawful with men and God.

Freedom or unfreedom may be taken in three forms:- 1, Lawless; 2, Lawful; 3, Circumstantial. Lawless freedom or license to do whatever a man will is by far too much of it, even for a king like Nero, in a community of men; and is fit only for the state of Robinson Crusoe with a right which there was none to dispute. I deem good and full freedom to be lawful and circumstantial freedom with which a man is both *lawfully* and *circumstantially* free to do a righteous act or not, since there is a mockery of freedom with which, while a man may be lawfully free in an act, others may constrain him in it by shackles of circumstances. In the fable of the division of the booty by the lion who hunted with other animals, his great-headed highness proclaimed that either of them was free to take the fourth share. He gave them lawful freedom to take it, but said the act would bring the share-taker under his anger, a circumstance that made his law-freedom a mockery, and held them in circumstantial thraldom against the taking of the share; and so in cases in which capital may most carefully forbear to restrain a man's freedom by an open act against the law, it may, if it will, restrain it by a thraldom of circum-stances, against which the law is utterly idle. The law allows a lawfully qualified man a vote for his representative in parliament; but capital which affords him bread by a work of one skill, in which he could hardly earn his livelihood else-where, may well afford to leave him the lion's law-freedom while it can hold him under the circumstantial thraldom of its anger, which would be the loss of his bread. If capital may choose to carry on some work on the Sabbath, and if a labourer wish to enjoy its bodily and spiritual blessings, capital may readily allow him his law right to freedom, and take it away by the circumstantial thraldom of a threat of dismissal.

The Prayer-book bids the clergyman catechise the children of his parish, but if he should gather those of the labourers under a mighty capital for his instruction, and capital objected to dogmatic teaching, it could afford to allow the rubric or canon all its law force, and send the children home with its circumstantial power over their fathers, so that in some cases Christian and canon and constitutional law are powerless against riches. Great capital goes far in the winning of monopoly, and if monopoly works against circumstantial freedom, so it is a tyranny.

If all the estates of a county were by any chance to be gathered into the hands of one capitalist, so that all but one of its freeholders should become tenants, or all the tenants labourers at will under him, it can hardly be doubted that they would be less free than they are now, by that one circumstantial bond of bread-affording capital. And if all the trade of one hundred free-stalled shoe-makers were gathered into the factory of one capital, and each of them should henceforth earn his pay of it, then, whereas heretofore every hour was his own, and he might break it at will for half-an-hour's talk with a welcome friend, or for air-taking in his garden, for affording his wife some little service of a strong pair of hands, for instructing his children's minds from some incident of the time, for looking at some sight, for listening to a tune of music, or for easing his limbs from the wearisomeness of work in one unhandy posture; so the capital-holden workman may be bound by the clock to his work, or by a watchman or timesman to the clock, till he has fulfilled, like a hireling, his day.

It may be replied that the untimed craftsman at home is holden to his work by the circumstantial tyranny of his own want of a livelihood, which is true; but he is not, like the hired labourer, bound to another's order or time; Master John may play for half-an-hour after two, and make it up by half-an-hour's work after six or eight, while hired John may have but little choice of time or tide.

That a monopoly of capital may be finding work for many hands may be true, but it is only so much of the truth as is favour of monopoly, for though it is true that where monopoly has made many hands takers of day wages, instead of holders of trades, it may be good that they should earn their wages rather than nothing; yet it may have been quite as well for them if the profit on their toil had been taken by themselves instead of the great capitalist, and if they had taken their money on their own desk rather than on the Saturday pay-table. We have known a case where there were ten or twelve master workmen, and where one with a capital drove the others out of their trade; then nine free-handed tradesmen sunk into the rank of less free workmen under his capital, or tried other callings for which they were little trained or qualified, and laboured for some time with the odds of skill against them. The kindness which is done by capital when it affords employment to people from whom, by a monopoly, it has taken their little businesses, is such as one might do to a cock by adorning his head with a plume made of feathers pulled out of his own tail.

It may be allowed that there are also truths of good to the community or capitalists on the side of great capital. They are of late become the theme of much congratulation. Be there such. I am not blaming the capitalist, but I am concerned in my writing of labour and gold to show the possible effect of the increase of great working-capitals and monopolies on the labourer's freedom or welfare.

Great working capital may be a great commercial help to the holder of it, but as hand-hiring capital it promotes monopoly, and leaves fewer free master workmen, and makes more on-hangers for bread on the will that wields it; and hirelingship is so seldom felt to be as good as mastership, that hardly a man would willingly lose his business, and work as a journeyman, as if his change were not from greater to less good; and few hirelings would be unwilling to take mastership, as if it were a falling and not a rising from hirelingship.

It is often said that the interest of capital and labour are identical, and so in truth they are as long as they are kept so by the law of Christian kindness; but if the truth, or the broad form of it, be misunderstood by the hand-hiring capital, it does not follow that the wealth of the capitalist and workman are identical. It has been declared by writers on behalf of capital at work in the West Indies, that its interest was advanced by the slavery of its labourers, and that it declined by their freedom, and it would be no new discovery to find that capital may increase faster in some cases with low than with high wages. It is true that a man may now leave his wife a million of money earned for him by workmen in the service of his capital, but then fewer men out of every hundred in his trade may leave their children a hundred pounds. The monopoly of great capital makes, between a hireling and a mastership in his business, a great gulf which is so hard to pass that it may discourage him from a struggle for it.

With the capital of a *turn* and a pair of hand-cards, a woman could formerly set up in carding and spinning: with the long building of three or four tiers of windows, and floor after floor laden with machinery, a woman cannot buy her machinery for her own house, and therefore she must go forth to wait on it. We knew an old man who had grown up in a neighbourhood of small holdings and farms, and had begun farming with a calf; he then won a cow, and afterwards a few others, with a little farm, and at last died a land-holder; but no labourer can hope to gain by any work or thrift, capital enough to stock a farm of a thousand a year, and so has no incitement to try.

Mr. Barton, at a Meeting of the Statistical Society in April, 1849, remarked that the rapid increase of crime since 1805, when the returns from the different courts of criminal justice were first collected and published, had naturally attracted the attention of those engaged in statistical researches; but it is admitted that the cause of this change in our social position is not yet thoroughly understood. The purport of this communication was to advert to one element of the question - the greater or less sub-division of the soil. He therefore divided the counties of England and Wales into five classes. The first class containing those counties where the average number of labourers to each occupier of land amounts to 2 or less, the second class from 2 to 3, the third from 3 to 5, the fourth from 5 to 7, the fifth more than 7. These numbers are taken from the population returns of 1831. Distributing the counties in this order, he then proceeded to estimate the prevalence of crime in each by comparing the average number of commitments in five years with the amount of population. He demonstrated that in every case the number of commitments rose regularly and progressively with the size of the farms. In the first class the number of commitments in each 100,000 of population amounted to 37, in the second class to 104, in the third class to 117, in the fourth class to 142, in the fifth class to 184. The result is that the possession of property, whether to a large of small amount, retains a man from breaking the laws of his country.

The ratio which expresses the comparative tendency to crime between the agricultural and manufacturing population is a follows:- In the first class the commitments are five times greater among the manufacturing than the agricultural population, in the second class nearly twice, in the third class more than twice; but in the large manufacturing towns a still higher amount of crime appears to prevail than in the manufacturing population of the counties at large. Thus the numbers of commitments in Liverpool, on an average of five years, 1839 to 1843, was equal to 238, or after applying the correction suggested by Mr. Nelson, 214 in 100,000.

The number of commitments in Manchester for 1841 were 411, or adopting Mr. Nelson's correction, 370 in each 100,000. This is the highest amount of crime that Mr. Barton had met with in any district, being ten times that which prevails in the yeomanry counties.

It has been objected against small farms and holdings that their occupiers, who would be men with very little capital and small theoretical knowledge, could not make the most of their land, as they could not till it fully and economically: and as they could not work their farmlings so productively as the more wealthy and intelligent occupier of the thousand acres, so they could not compete with him in the market without a loss by which they must at last be driven out of it, and off their lands.

This reasoning I cannot so readily understand. Let it be allowed that it may require a capital of £8. to work an acre of land; then ten acres would require £80., a hundred acres £800., and a thousand acres £8000. Why could not a man with £800. work a hundred acres as productively as another with £8000. could till a thousand acres? or why would not a tenth of a capital work a tenth of its land? It may be objected to this that occupiers of small farms could not afford to buy and keep expensive agricultural machines; and to this it might be answered again that a machine which one man might not afford to buy, five may keep or hire among them. This is incontrovertible, since threshing machines and drilling machines have been so engaged among holders of farms.

Take it in another light. Is it not true that there are actually occupiers of small farmlings, or Cincinnati, of four acres, now competing with the large holder, and upon a higher rent than he pays? Is it not true that the market gardeners near London or other large towns, or the spade-tillers of garden allotments, make as much out of half an acre as is produced by a half acre of a contiguous farm? and that they can afford to give as high a rent per acre as the farmer of their parish? Is it not true that their spade and rake bring more per acre from the land than is produced by the plough and harrow?

Labour is capital, and if a working family holding a small farm, have a father and two sons at work, then they have the capital equal to the wages of three labourers in labour instead of money; and if it be objected that they are taking the labour out of the hands, and therefore the bread out of the mouth of three labourers, it may be answered, (if such an objection is worth answering,) that as such men could not occupy a large farm, and therefore could not be farmers without a small farm, therefore we must conclude that their labour in farming while it takes up the work of three labourers, keeps them or takes them out of the rank of labourers, and therefore it lessens the competitive labourers as much as it lessens the call for their labour.

DIVISION OF LABOUR AND SKILL

SOME kind of division of labour is of good, or else none would long hold its place in labour of any kind. It is found in the hauling of hay that it is better that one man should pitch and another should load, than that each of the two should climb up to place in his own hay; and in house building that a bricklayer should work on with the bricks and mortar brought up to him by a man of less hand-skill, than that he should take his hands from their craftwork to fetch himself his materials. Now the division of the work of hay-loading may be a bare division of labour and not of skill, as the pitcher of one day may be the loader of another, and the two men may have equal skill in loading or pitching; but the division of the work of the bricklayer and hodman may hold on in a division of skill or a permanent division of labour.

The good of a division of labour or skill is a good for the working capital or the work, rather than for the workman, for the far-driven division of labour in the form of a division of skill in many of our handicrafts may bring some evils on the labourer. The first evil to the workman, as a man, is an evil of the very good for which labour is divided, that it makes him a man of only one skill, and so narrows the sphere within which he may win his livelihood. By keeping to one division of much-divided labour a man wins a readiness of hand which increases the speed of his work, but then it leaves him hanging for bread upon a continuance of the circumstances in which only that underdivision of labour will yield a man bread.

By division of labour in pin-making, a pin-header wins great quickness in his little division of work, but then, asunder from the pin factory or his fellow pinmakers, he has a hand of a skill that is utterly worthless for bread. He may be as a helpless child in the world of colonial or common labour; and a village carpenter and wheelwright with his many skills of house and waggon building, wheelmaking, and painting, has a better hand for a livelihood as an emigrant or travelling workseeker, than that of a man who, by a keen division of labour has only the one skill of spoke-shaving or French-polishing, and who therefore is confined to business-es and towns of a certain magnitude. I have known, in a factory, of a case in which the work of a boy was barely the turning of a wheel, a work by which he could never become better qualified to do his own life a service in a more direct way than by earning of money.

Whatever may be the trade or business of men in the Philippines, we are told near-ly all of them can build themselves *Nipa* houses, or houses of Nipa grass or attap, on a bamboo framework, or wooden pillars; but few of our one-skilled craftsmen who are not of the building trades could build themselves houses; and an English writer on Australia would warn the one-skilled English emigrant that he should not rashly set his hands to house-building unless it is his craft. He says:- "When a man has money, it will be found cheaper to contract for a hut than to spend time in learning how to work the Australian timber, which, at first, is very awkward, even to an experienced European carpenter."

The Malays (Osborn's Quedah) perform with great readiness, by their little adze or axe (for they can set it for either of the tools), jobs of boat-building, house-building, and other timber work, which would in England be the work of several skills, and at which a man of one skill would be sorely puzzled. A writer on Australia says:- "One settler's wife was an excellent milker, her next door neigh-bour could not manage a cow: an agreement was made much to the advantage of both, settler A was to bail up and milk B's cows, while B in return agreed to give one hour's instruction daily in reading and writing to A's children." An excellent plan with these two women's lucky near-neighbourhood: but if they had been wide asunder it would have been better for them if each had known how to milk, as well as to read and write.

The division of skill or labour is much upholden among the Hindoos, not only by the castes, but among the Soodurs themselves; as a servant, whatever time he may have on his hands, does not choose to take the work of any skill but his own, whence it becomes needful that those who hire hand-service should keep more ser-vants than they would need with our less distributed servant's work. It does not seem to be universally true that division of skill is of good service to work itself. The old masters in painting, ground and formed their own colours, and it is not allowed that they were worse in pureness or wear than those which are now given by division of skill in a form ready for the painter's palette; nor is it thought that sundry kinds of food and drink which are now sent into our houses by division of skill, are more wholesome than those that were made under the roofs of our forefathers by hands of several skills.

Another evil of far-driven division of skill is often that of impaired health. That a man may become and continue, for his time, perfect as a physical being, he needs a nearly equal action of the muscles and limbs of his body, and it is an evil of division of skill that it often holds a man to one kind of action of one or of a few of his limbs, while the others are less worked, or wholly inactive; or that it holds him too long in one position, or in an unhandy one, or in an unwholesome place, so that the reaction of his work, unchecked by any counteraction of timely change, affects for evil the form, and action and health of his body.

A medical professor, in a lecture delivered before the College of Surgeons, bade his audience observe how often, as they listened to him, they shifted the weight of their bodies to relieve the portions that had been cramped. "Were you constrained" he said, "to retain one position during the whole hour, you would rise stiff and lame." "I have seen," says Mr. Forbes, in speaking of the Indian jogees, "a man who had made a vow to hold up his arms above his head, and never to suspend them. At length he totally lost the power of moving them at all. His arms, from having been so long in one position were become withered and dried up." The Guachos of South America, who are almost always on horseback, and going over the ground with little labour of limb, though they hold their legs constantly or much in the action of the grip, become bow-legged and bad walkers, and worse runners, so that they often fall down, like children not yet strong on foot. "The Barotse tribe of boatmen," says Dr. Livingstone, "have large deeply developed chests and shoulders, with indifferent lower extremities."

So some callings affect for the worse the form of the body, or the state of the skin or lungs; and in some cases a man's figure will show his trade. Some nations and men have understood that the Allwise himself has willed some division of skill by the sexes, though our division of it has now in some cases, thwarted what has been deemed to be the Divine plan. It seems as if man had in his hands the defence of his life and rights, and the winning of food, as by hunting, farming, and handicrafts and commerce; and that woman was to hold the lighter indoor works of a fine hand guided by fancy, the making of apparel, and the adorning of the abode; and so our Saxon speech seems to have been quite right, when, on the pen of King Alfred, it called the male sex the *spear sex,* and the women the *spindle sex;* and when it called a wife *seo wif,* the weaver, or *seo wifman,* the weaving-man, and a girl a *spinster*, a spinner, as in those times women were the makers of the outer adornings of the body, while men were handlers of the spear. But now the spindle, the shuttle, and the yarn, are often taken out of the hand of women, unless they are drawn from their houses to the factory, where they lose the learning of the many skills of the housewife for the one skill of the joining of a thread, or the setting of a bobbin, or one of the division of the clothing labour, and the handling of cloth, women's as well as men's, and the making up of millinery, are often in the hands of men, and women are left with too few openings for making a livelihood by work fit for their sex. It is true that in compensation for this loss of what seems more like their own work, we see women at work in the field, as they may be seen among tribes of Africa and some other nations; but the Tonga men held that it was not consistent with feminine character to do hard work. "Who loves a masculine woman?" they would ask.

MEASURE AND QUANTITY OF LABOUR

LABOUR is the measure of commercial value, but it is not easy to find what, besides commercial value, can be taken as.a handy measure of labour. It may be deemed that as a cause may be measured by its effect, so labour may be measured by its work: but labour is both *action* and its reaction; and work, which is the effect only of the action, cannot therefore be a fair measure of its *reaction.*

It is not the same quantity of labour to carry a box through a passage filled with flames or smoke, and one of cool or clear air; or to row a boat half-a-mile on the bright face of a pretty river, and waters that give off a sickening vapour. And even work itself is no measure of labour unless its quality as well as its quantity be taken into the rating. A piece of canvas or cheesecloth and a piece of fine linen, of equal surface or weight, may not be woven by equal quantities of labour; nor would equal quantities of labour bore through a yard of chalk and of limestone, or saw through a square foot of deal and oak, or carry a weight a hundred yards on a level and up hill.

Time, again, has been taken as a measure of labour, but it is not always a truthful one, as the action of the labour may vary or differ in intensity and effect. Where the intensity of the action can be forestated, or is needfully constant, time is not a bad measure of it, and so the labour of men is often rated by the hour, day, week, or year; but in some cases of time-rating the uncertainty of the action and the desire of the hirer to keep up its intensity, has brought upon the labourer scoldings, and the overseer or task-master; and on the slave, the whip. Where labour can be measured by the work, the labourer is well relieved from clock service, and both he and his employer from the evils of an uncertain intensity by piece work or tut work; but this again often brings in wranglings and anger upon questions of the quality of work.

The untrustworthiness of time, as a measure of labour, has been shown in a comparison which a writer has made of the work of an English and a Hindoo bricklayer. He says, "A single English bricklayer and hodman could, in one day, do the work of a dozen rajees, rundess and all. One would imagine from this that building was a very expensive process in India, but the contrary is the case. An English bricklayer and hodman will cost from eight to ten shillings a day, while the Indian *raj* and his two attendant *rundees* will not cost more than threepence or fourpence per day." - *Edinburgh Journal,* May, 1851.

The rating of labour by bare quantity of work has been taken up cunningly by makers, and not wisely by buyers of cheap or low-priced wares and adulterated goods, which, though they may bring the labourer money, can win him but little honour, and which cheat the buyer with a name and an appearance of a commodity instead of a good service, like the cheap razors which were made only to sell. Thence the market is furnished with clothing stuffs of little price and less wear; with drawers formed by glue instead of dove-tailing and good joinery; with gilding done by diluted instead of leaf-gold; with ware of base alloy for silver; with food which feeds not or is unwholesome; and, in fine, with a show of greater labour where less is bestowed. This falsehood of labour is owing to a yearning after wares of good name and kind, for low prices, among buyers; and an over-strained competition among makers; and unless it is checked it may lessen the sale of our goods in foreign markets.

The rating of horse-labour or horse-power in an engine takes in time, weight, and space, as one horse-power is that power which will raise 33,000 pounds weight one foot in a minute. There are some cases of the labour of motion, where it is well measured by space, as the labour of railway companies in the carrying of passengers at so much a mile. And though it is true that the labour of carrying *Mr. Little* may not be the same as that of carrying *Mr. Big,* yet the company wisely take the average of the different weights, and hold that "a man's a man for a' that," and so leave weight out of their rating; though, in the hauling of goods, they measure their labour by weight and space.

OVERWORK, &c.

AS it is no easy thing to find a measure, otherwise than that of commercial value, for labour itself, so it is hard to define what is the quantity of labour which affords the true labour's good, and is neither overwork or underwork for the health of man; and in truth, there is reason to believe that the good quantity of labour for one climate may be a bad one in another, though we can hardly help believing that a man may be overworked, as well as underworked, for his health.

By a wise ordinance of the Allwise it seems that labour is easier and more welcome to a man in the climate where more of it is needful for his life-gear. In England we need a greater quantity of bedding and clothing and firing, or of the warmth of it, than men do in Africa or Greece, since, owing to the greater warmth of Africa or Greece, the African needs little more than a loin-girdle and shoulder-piece, and the Greek can sleep in a rug in the open air; and so far England calls for more labour than Africa or Greece: but then in the lower heat of England the heat of action may be less irksome than in the warmer lands, and man can bear more labour.

I should guess that the good quantity of labour for man's health would be little more than that which would win him all needful life-gear for his climate, without pernicious luxuries, or without gear which is needless otherwise than to pride or vice, and without calls on his labour for the life-gear of classes unworking in any way for the community; and if we take time as a measure of the good quantity of labour one cannot well deem it to be more than that of the daylight of his land, or half his time.

Our Saviour says, "The night cometh, when no man can work," which, of the work of men in some forms of life is now true, as I believe it is as true that a man cannot, without more of less harm to his health, work from year to year through more of his life-time than that of his daylight, or of half of it. King Alfred was most likely wise in his timing of his labour, as in many other things, when he allowed eight hours for work, eight for godly and intellectual exercises, and eight for rest and food; though the good quantity of a man's labour would vary with its intensity, its sameness or variation, or its reaction; and inaction is as bad as overwork. Techell, Dr. Livingstone's friend, the African chief, who had been rather thin from good action in the chase, when he set himself closely to his book on learning to read, became quite corpulent for the want of exercise; and by a benificent ordinance of our Maker, there is crowded into one hour of rest after many hours of useful toil, a greater quantity of pure pleasure, as a happy reaction to labour, than may have been perceived through many hours of inaction.

If we say that because we have candle-light and gas-light therefore we have in them new calls, as they are new helps, to work, we go to prove too much; for since with daylight and artificial light we may have unceasing light, so we have a call to work continuously, which will not stand good, as would be found upon trial. From a holding of time as a measure of labour, and even from a right opinion of the waste of time in inaction or idleness, we may, however, at last so associate time with labour as to have a very low opinion of it:- that time is only a kind of stuff with which we may work and make gain. Not, like Saint Paul, to know Christ; not, like Timothy, to know God's word; not, like the naturalist, to know His works; not, like the old philospher, to refine one's mind by pure wisdom; not, like King Alfred, to make others more happy, or to refreshen his mind for fulfilling oncoming duties; not like an old Englishman, to cherish the bond of kindred love by cheerful leisure at the hearth:- but only to work, to trade, and get money.

"Time, which an Englishman values as money," says a writer (*Edinburgh Journal,* May, 1851), "has a very secondary place in the estimation of the Oriental." It may have in his estimation a secondary place as money, but not as health or happiness, for the Hindoos have a Shaster, the *Waeesheeshik,* on the fitness of time in action. "Time," says Mr. Squiers, on Nicaragua, "in these regions is not regarded as of much importance, and everything is done very leisurely;" but then some think that from the over-high opinion of the money-value of time in the United States, some things, such as the important one of eating itself, are done too hastily, and that from lack of time for chewing and digestion of food, and rest of body and mind, the health of the American constitution is already much impaired, and

"To earn more wealth, and mar your men,
Is to kill the golden-egged hen."

For the health of our bodies and minds it is to be feared that some classes of Englishmen are overworked, and a weekly half-holiday would be a boon for the health and happiness of a degenerating class of labourers, and we believe no less an one to others. If there be such a thing as overwork, then it is clear that the man under its effects will be sooner worn out of labour, and in England sooner thrown on the poor's-rate. But what is to be done? I cannot, says a master craftsman, afford to give a half-holiday to my thirty or forty men, unless I take up from each of them a half-day's wages or charge it to my employers. Things would right themselves in time. If I now pay two pounds a year to the poor's-rate for the early decay of over-worked labourers, what should I lose if I paid their employer two pounds a year more for the holiday, and their longer wear relieved me of it in the rate? It is not the quality of evil to bear good fruit.

That the time of work in our shops and places of congregated labour is often too long, must be felt from the workpeople's joy in the breath and freedom of the open air, on a holiday, and often from their wanness and weakness; and if all tradesmen could restrain the tyranny of competition, and close the eyelids of their shops in earlier rest, none would lose money by it, since, as men who formerly were behind the starting time of coaches that would wait for them are now in time for the unwaiting train, and so the train loses no more custom than the coaches; so if all shops were closed an hour earlier, late buyers would be earlier ones by an hour.

REACTION OF LABOUR, AND OF INACTION

THE reaction of inaction on the mind and body, is hardly less harmful than that of the worst kinds of action. The reaction of an inaction of limb and senses in a dark cell has been deemed too bad to be long enforced on a criminal, and one may fairly conceive that laziness or confinement might with-hold a man's limbs from action till he could hardly wield them.

Inaction of body tends to breed weakness, deficient action of lungs, and aëration of the blood, indigestion, irritability of the nerves, and the seeds of may diseases; while the tendency of inaction of the mind is to afflict it with weakness or silliness, and moodiness or madness.

GOOD REACTION OF LABOUR. - The reaction of some kinds of action of body and mind is pleasing and wholesome, and the labour of such action is in those cases to be rated as the difference of the effects, for evil, of the action and reaction; and, indeed, in some such cases, the labour is not so rightly called labour or work as play or sport, or recreation, or a pursuit. The action of a day's cricketing, or boating, or hunting, or shooting, may be as intense as that of a good day's work; but its reaction on the mind is so sweetly beguiling, that it may wholly cancel the action, and its labour may be reckoned zero.

The reaction of inaction becomes so dreadful after a time, that men with that gift which many of us are to ready to desire,- empty time, not seldom shun their oncoming misery in the most silly, or even vicious and pernicious pursuits of idleness, and therefore it is a happiness that minds should be informed in youth, by an insight into the world of art and knowledge, or that they should in later life be quickened, through grace, to the pursuit of some healthy labour of mind, though it be one at which the world, in ignorance of the links of labour by which great ends are sometimes attained, may laugh, as a useless though harmless hobby. As the steam-engine is at the later end of a chain of hobbies beginning with Hiero's toy, so the once despised labours of the entomologist may yet lead to discoveries of great blessing in the economy of man-needed food and man-bred poisons.

Against the bad reaction on the body of bodily inaction, or the insufficient action of some indoor callings, it is needful that all populations should have time and place for athletic games, among which one of the best and noblest is our game of cricket, which, for its entertainment of the mind, its quickening of the sight, and the equal and full action of all the limbs and muscles, is worth all the Olympic games, and a timely antidote to many of the evils of our division of labour.

Work of free skill is less irksome and better than constrained hand work of no effectual thought, such as that of continual turning of a wheel, or churning of butter; and it is more healthy to rack one's mind in effectual devices to win a skilful end, than to work as a machine without a free aim or thought; and so, as a Hindoo poet says, to be like a smith's bellows, breathing without life. Even in needful labour it should be borne in mind that the action of the compulsory labour of the unfree is of worse reaction than the same quantity of chosen labour, that may be left off at will.

"There is perhaps," says Mr. Dunn, "no class of men on the earth who lead a life of more continued exertion (action), danger, and excitement (reaction), and who are more enamoured of their occupations, than the free trapper of the wild regions of the west (of North America): with his horse and his rifle he is independent of the world and spurs its restraints." The Canadian Indians (*teste* Mr. Joutel) were fond of freedom; they preferred their own way of life to that of Europeans, and said that if they had fewer conveniences, they had less toil in winning of them, and consequently had more time to themselves. "The savage of New Holland, however well fed and treated, longs, after a time, for the freedom and laziness of his former life. He has little to admire in the life of the white servant, toiling day after day for his food and wages, enjoying no corobory, no basking in the sun - in short, no freedom."

This view of the sweet or good reaction of some kinds of action would show us the true cases of some pursuits of the mind in science, learning, and the fine arts. The action of the botanist, naturalist, or antiquary, is lost under the joy of the new discovery, the confirmation of the hopeful theory, and the prospective good of the mind's labours. The pleasure of embodying the soul-quickening thoughts in sweet speech, or in thrilling harmony, or in forms and colours of heavenly loveliness, beguiles the poet, the musician, and the painter, not only of their art, but, for a time, of the ills of life. And after all, men of genius may be wise to bear this truth in mind, that they have some reward in the reaction of their labour, if it is ill-rewarded by the world; so that if low labours of bad reaction on body or mind may win more money, they can hardly make amends for the evil of a reaction which may be deadly pernicious to body or soul.

The labour of the swindler, thief, and forger, the over-reacher, and the adulterator of food, may be slight and well paid in money; but the reaction, if not on the body in the way of punishment, yet on the soul in the way of fear, or uneasiness, or the warping of the judgement, and the blunting of the conscience, and the ill-will of men, and guilt with God, is such as to leave a vast balance of evil rather than of good in the wealth of sinful toil. As there is a good reaction of action on the mind, so there is by the divine Providence a good reaction of it on the body. Not only is action of the lungs and limbs needful for upholding the health of the body, but it increases the might and worksomeness of the working limbs. Man gains swiftness of foot by running, strength of arms by wielding them, power of body by work, and skill by art.

DIGNITY AND DISDAIN OF WORK

HAND-LABOUR is the lot of man, his main, if not only true wealth, and the upholder of his life; and markworthy, therefore, is the disdain of it among many, if not most nations, and especially among those who have most of its fruit in the form of wealth. Men like to be thought unworking, to have a pair of hands that are useless for the winning of life-gear, and bootless to other men; and despise the doers of the work, without which the State could not be upholden a year, and they could not live a week. Thence the pride of a soft hand, and among the Chinese of fingernails outgrown into claws, as an evidence of unworkingness, and sometimes among ourselves, an affected ignorance of the most useful kinds of labour. I recollect to have said once on a summer's day to a young lady who had been bred up in the midst of grass fields, that it was fine weather for the haymaking; and her answer was, "Ah! I dare say it may be; I know nothing of haymaking:" affecting ignorance of what has been the main wealth of England from the time of the old Britons to our own - the grass and hay, with the cattle of the island; though a maxim of Bacon is, that whatever is worthy of being, is worthy of knowing.

I have fancied that were it not for the kindness of woman, disdain of labour may enact a funny scene at a house - such as that a lady, Mrs. Malmust, might be sitting in her room in a pelting storm of snow or hail, and may see through a window that her friend Mrs. Mahrook is at the door; she rings the bell that the maid, who happens to be at the top of the house, may open the door, as it is beneath herself to do such work. The maid does not hear the bell, and the mistress, seeing her friend shivering and shrinking, and stamping with cold feet, rings the bell still harder, and at last breaks the bell-rope, and then runs upstairs to fetch the maid for the unworthy work of doorkeeper, and at last greets her nose-frozen friend with such words as "Oh! my dear Mrs. Mahrook, I am so grieved to find that you were kept so long at the door, and in such weather!"

Xenophon says that Socrates held labour to be a good, and idleness an evil, and spoke of those whom he saw doing any good as good workmen, and of gamblers and evil-doers as idle men; as Hesiod had sung, "There is no disgrace in work, the disgrace is in idleness." So Socrates in his dialogue with Aristarchus on Want, asks him if he is not aware that several of his friends get an income by handywork. "Certainly," he replies, "but they have barbarian slaves whom they can compel to do fitting work, but I have in my house freemen and kinsfolk." "Well then," he replied, "If you have in your house only free people and kinsfolk, do you think they should do nothing but eat and sleep?" The Christian law is, that if any man will not work, neither should he eat; for the rich can work as well as the poor, with their thought, their office, their influence, or their deeds.

Along with disdain of labour we find a pride of its fruits, - wealth; the bliss of idle pride seems to be the knowledge that he works for nobody, but that many work for him, as if the greatest among men were the one who does least for others and has most others doing service to him; whereas our Saviour says, "Let him who will be greatest among you be your servant," as the greatest Christian is he who does greatest service of hand or mind to others, as Christ came not to be ministered unto, but to minister.

The rich men of a tribe in Africa (*teste* Dr. Livingstone), wear a load of ornaments on their legs, and walk astride that one leg may clear the other; and so then, forsooth, the less rich with fewer ornaments walk astraddle that they may walk like a gentleman, or may seem to have worn legloads of ornaments. The Bechuanas (Livingstone), who are rich enough to mingle curd in their meal porridge, cast on the poor or weak the reproach that they are mere water-porridge men.

Disdain of labour and pride of wealth are breeding among us great evils of social life. Miss Tossnoddle will marry only a man who can keep her in costly idleness, and Mr. Knittbrow will only marry a wife with a fortune; and thence God's true wedlock, grounded on the love of excellence and loveworthiness, if often lost, and in its stead we have a train of evils, physical and moral, which are increasing at a frightful rate. Why should not young people choose the excellent in their mates, and put their hands boldly and faithfully to the work of life; doing their daily duty to the state to which God has called them, and taking his daily bread, and inward peace, and the other blessings which He bestows on well-doing.

DESPISED AND HONOURED CRAFTS

ON taking a wide view of the feeling of nations, we find it hard to assume any constant rule on which sundry crafts and labours are despised and honoured among men. It would seem a rational rule that labours which are of most need or service to men, should be holden in greatest honour; but nothing can be more needful or of more service to men's lives than tillage or farming, the labours for *feorm,* an old word for food; and yet the labourers on the ground are usually classed very low in the scale of life. The Romans held the art in high honour. "Than agriculture," says Cicero, "nothing is better, nothing more pleasing." They deemed it a pursuit worthy of the highest of their nobles, and the greatest of their senators; and it is said in a Saxon dialogue that farming holds the headship of all worldly crafts, because the tiller feeds us all; but yet, although the Saxons held the craft in honour, they esteemed very lightly many of its working hands, as they were slaves or serfs. We honour fair trade, but some of the African tribes, like the Romans, rate trade much lower than tillage: as Dr. Livingstone's men, on being told that the Portuguese traders imported corn, cried out, "Are they ignorant of tillage? They know nothing but buying and selling; they are not men."

To the Egyptians a shepherd was abominable; but with the Israelites the feeding of sheep or kine was not beneath the highest-born sons of the land; and I have known a daughter of a rich settler in Africa who retained her rank and refinement of mind while she wielded the crook over a flock at the Cape. Mr. Sydney, however, says of the stockman in Australia:- "The pursuits of an Australian stockman carry one back to Scythian times, or Tartar countries, except that he dwells in a wooden hut instead of a tent; but he lives on horseback, and all his hopes and ambitions are centred in cattle. He neither ploughs nor sows, and despises those who do; his food is beef, and his pride is in his horse; above all, he scorns a 'crawling shepherd.'"

In England, Ceres is far from granting of equal honours to her votaries, for the owner of the land ranks before the man who tills it with his capital, and he who tills it with his capital is above the labourer who tills it with his hands; and so low has been holden the rank of the serf tiller of the land that *villain, villanus,* an old name for a serf labourer, is now become a word of stinging reproach. Then, again, the iron-smith was in so high esteem among the old Welsh that a smith was much honoured and needfully free by his very craft, which no slave, as such, could hold; whereas, in Abyssinia and in *El Hejaz,* the blacksmith is vile, if not an outcast. Among the Maidan Arabs, owing to their good principle of hospitality, it is most disgraceful to sell bread; and with some tribes, as the Somal (Layard), a *babban,* or milk-seller, is a man of very bad reputation.

With Tonga men, formerly, the lowest classes were cooks and shavers and men of unskilled labour, while the building of canoes and the making of weapons were crafts of high honour and of the highest classes, though with us the shipwright or gunsmith has little honour above the so taken viler crafts of the Tonga men. When, in the time of Horace Walpole, a daughter of a noble house married a dramatic performer, she was felt to have sunk utterly out of all worthiness of her order; but when a nobleman, some years afterwards, married a rich lady who had been an actress, the glory of his rank was not dimmed by the slightest shade of disgrace.

At the court of the old Welsh kings, the mead-brewer took precedence of the physician by one place; though in England, in our days, the physician is placed ahead of the beer-vat into the learned professions. With the Egyptians, the dissector, who did the needful service of opening, with a knife, the body for embalming, fled away under stones and curses from the bystanders; though with us the surgeon goes forth in peace from a *post-mortem* examination. Among the Tonga men the funeral rites were the work of the nobles or highborn classes, though we should greatly wonder to read on a shop sign, "His Grace the Duke of Duncragmore, Undertaker."

In England, the man who handles a settled business is more respectable than the one who rambles in his craft. An iron-smith lowers himself to a tinker if he roams with his tools, and if a tradesman lifts his shop on wheels and migrates with it from town to town, or carries his wares from house to house, he usually sinks into a less esteemed class of tradesmen, the hawkers; for the word *Hawker,* like the feminine *Huckster* (Hawkster), seems to mean, by etymon, *Hedge-trader,* and had been a word of reproach. And yet a tradesman may go forth to sell goods by sample, if not by bulk, and retain his higher respectability under the name of a commercial traveller.

An intelligible rule for the esteem of callings would be that labour, which works most for the welfare of man, should be the most highly esteemed, and that those which only win wealth to the labourer without yielding a corresponding good to those from whom the wealth is drawn, should be less esteemed: but there is no such rule, for a cunning and successful trader in the shares of swindling companies may be as much esteemed as a farmer, or builder, or weaver, or tanner.

It would not seem an unreasonable rule, moreover, if men-labourers were lightly esteemed with women's work in their hands: but here, again, opinion is wild, a man might bring on himself a reproach of effeminacy if he took up the needle as a maker of baby-linen, and yet he may take up some other kinds of labour that as clearly belong to the mind and hands of women without any such disgrace as the distaff and spindle would have carried into the hands of men among the Greeks or Romans. The word *obstetrix* is only the title of a woman, and with the eastern nations, as among the Romans, her office is kept in women's hands; but with our greater refinement in science, we have ceased to regard with shame the action of a man in an office which many other people hold most sacred to womanhood.

One of the evils of slavery in a community is that the slaveholders hand over to the slaves many of the most needful kinds of labour, which, therefore, as the work of slaves, fall into evil repute and lie under the scorn of the free men; and so, if labours of skill are left to the slaves, the free may become proud, but idle and unskilled dolts, with little energy but that of fighting, and with little power for the winning of greatness but that of the sword, which soon grows weak unless it is backed by the resources of labour-won wealth. So the Turks with Greeks in their hands, and the Americans with blacks under their lash, are rising to greatness less rapidly than states of only free labour; and when Aristarchus, of whom Xenophon writes in his "Memorabilia," was grieving that his narrow income would not afford a living for his destitute kinswomen in the time of the disturbances, and when Socrates recommended him to some kinds of work, such as those with which some of his neighbours were thriving, he answered that they had slaves set to work, but he had *free people.*

From the Roman ideas of occupations which became freemen *(liberi)* as distinct from slaves, we have our name of the so-called *Liberal* Arts, in Latin *Artes Liberales,* or *Freemen's Arts.* In our English minds, at least, the respectability of crafts is much enhanced by wealth, so that a man who works a craft with a great capital and other men's hands, is deemed more respectable than he who works it with his own hands, and those of his children. An uncle is at once lifted to a respectable rank by the statement of his niece that he is in such or such a trade in a very large way; and if "Willie brew'd a peck o' ma't" at a brewing, he was not worthy to be ranked with the brewer whose heavy-steeded drays are rumbling forth on all roads. The spinning of flax with a wheel was disreputable, as weighed against the craft of spinning by the owner of the fifty-windowed or thousand-spindled factory; and shoemaking on one pair of knees is not to be ranked with that of the master tradesman who keeps on twenty lapstones; nor is the market gardener or the tiller of four acres of ground brother to the many- teamed farmer of hundreds of acres of land. A huckster is not a grocer, a pedler is not a merchant, a carpenter is not a builder, a stall is not a shop, nor a shop an establishment.

MACHINERY

A TOOL acts by the hand, and a machine acts by more than the hand; and while a tool is a help of the workman, as such, a machine is a help to the owner's capital rather than his hand. It has been already stated that there is no gain of labour by a tool or machine unless all the labour of which it relieves the owner be more than all the labour which brought it to hand.

The objective good of a machine or tool may be conceived to be of several forms:-
1. That it shortens or lessens labour: but since a lessening of labour may itself be

conceived of sundry forms, it may be right to distinguish one from another. A machine may be conceived to lessen labour if it lessens the time of the action, or performs a given piece of work in less time; as if a man could reap with a sickle half-an-acre of wheat in a day, and could mow with a wheat-scythe two acres of it in a day; where the scythe would lessen the time of the work of cutting the field of wheat.

This good, however, may not be a lessening of labour in the main, since a machine is itself a work of labour, and it may so happen that all the labour which brought a machine to hand, together with the labour of working with it, may be equal to the labour which would have done all its work as well without it; and so (2) the next way in which a machine can be conceived to lessen labour, is that the machine, reckoned as the labour which brought it to hand, with the labour that works with it, is less than all the labour which will do all its work as well without it.

3. Another lessening of labour is a lessening of labour to the workman, or such a lessening of it that a workman with the machine can do the same work with less action or bad reaction. A man with a stock and bit may bore a hole with less action than with a gimlet; while a toasting fork in one's hand may increase that action of holding the bread by its own weight, but may lessen the painful reaction of the heat on the hand; as a glove may increase the action of grasping and wielding a bill-hook, by its stiffness and weight, but may lessen the bad reaction of the thorns or gorse on the fingers.

The opinion that a machine lessens labour in the main, or yields life-gear to people for less labour or money, may not be true; and the mistake of it has bred hatred and the lawless breaking of machines by labourers on one side, and has drawn from others unbounded and, therefore, undue praise of machinery. A machine itself is labour, as it is brought to hand by labour, and will cost labour's worth; and the labour that does all the work of a machine is the labour that brought the machine to hand, together with all the labour spent on the work along with it; and has been stated (4th case of transference), unless the labour for which circumstances call on the buyer of the machine be diminished by more or not less than the labour that brought the machine to hand, there is no gain or diminution of labour by it.

If a machine be of wood and iron, then the very land which yielded the wood and iron was won by labour in the form of war, or money, or labour's worth; and for the wood again, there is the felling and sawing, and for the iron the mining, smelting, casting, and forging, and for both there is carriage, with all the compound labour of the hands and tools that made the machine; and all that labour has been spent on the work of the machine when it begins to act on it; and so all the labour that brought the machine to hand, together with the labour that works with it, may not be less than the labour which would have done its work without it. That this is yet the case with the threshing machine, is pretty clear from the fact that the price for threshing a bushel of wheat by the machine has been the same as that for the same work by flail. Wherever this is the case, labour in the main is not lessened by a machine, and the public gain nothing in cheapness by it.

The workmen's hatred of machinery has arisen from an insight into only half the truth, as they find that work is done by less labour with the machine, but overlook the labour that brought the machine to hand. If up to the beginning of last year ten thousand men had been employed on a kind of work without machines, and then in the last year four thousand were employed for making the machines, and six in working with them, they would not lessen the call for workmen, - though, in truth, they might tend to derange the labour market for a short time, - since the men displaced from their work by the machine are not at once qualified by skill to go back to the other end of the labour, and make the machine that is to do the work from which their hands have been displaced.

Machinery transfers rather than lessens labour. I want to see, but cannot find, that machinery lessens labour, and that it lessens it so far that it sends home the labourer to his wife and children, and his garden, or rest, and book, and friendly talk, an hour earlier in the evening, and until I see this happy effect of it, I cannot welcome it as a great good. Labourers make with machinery a no shorter, if they do not make a longer, day's work for their bread than their forefathers made for theirs without machinery, and it has drawn into its grasp the bodies of young children, till it was loosened by the Factory Bill.

It may be said that the public have the advantage of the lessening of labour by machinery, which, if machinery does not lessen labour, cannot be true. But who is that Proteus, the public? It seems as if every man were the public when he wanted an accommodation from the working classes, who, he would believe, are bound to accommodate him; but as soon as another wants an hardly-afforded accommodation from him, he feels that he is a private Englishman, and, as such, he has a right to manage his business at his own will. Workers at any craft are of the public, as well as others; but if by the public are meant those who buy the work of machinery, then if it comes by less labour to them, so since they win life-gear by less labour, they may rest from toil earlier in the evening, and yet we see that all classes of the public work for their life-gear, nowithstanding machinery, as hard or as long as did their forefathers without it, a token that machinery does not lessen labour. What then is the good of it? The main good of machinery seems to be that although it does not always do a given quantity of work by less labour in the main, it can do it in less time, by a form of accumulated or stored labour.

A machine is in labour what a Leyden battery is in electricity. A machine is a labour-battery, in which a quantity of labour is collected (*teste* the cost of it), so that it may be directed at will on a quantity of work, and do it in a time much shorter that that which would be taken up by unstored hand labour; and this in many cases, as in that of the need of printing thousands of newspapers in two or three hours, or of threshing a rick of wheat in a day, is an accommodation so great that those who need it are willing to buy it at the full price of unstored hand-labour.

Another argument in favour of machinery is that it does better work than that of the hand and hand-tools. Now, as it is not easy to define a measure of labour, so it is hardly more easy to define quality of work, since the goodness of work lies in strength or wearsomeness, in endurance of mechanical or chemical agencies, in fineness or smallness, in fitness and fittingness, in form and colour, and other qualities; and it may so happen that while a machine gives its work more of one good quality it may give it less of another.

A machine is a blind worker. It cannot vary its action for sudden variations of circumstances, like the mind-wielded hand. Its does its work neither worse nor better; as a barrel organ may not make mistakes, but it cannot make its air the speech of a living and yearning soul, like the hands of a rapt musician.

At a meeting of the Society of Arts (as reported in the *Athenæum*, Number 1272), Mr. Owen Jones, who was in the chair, observed that, "with all the artists of England with whom he was acquainted, as well as with foreign visitors, he found but one opinion, that the Indian and Tunisian articles (the work of rude hand-looms) were the most perfect in design of any that had appeared in the Exhibition. The opportunity of studying them had been a boon to the whole of Europe."

Mr. McMicking says of the Piña cloth of Manilla, "There is, perhaps, no more curious, beautiful, and delicate specimen of manufactures produced in any country than the Piña cloth (the work of less complex machinery than ours), which is made of a kind of hemp from the bark of a kind of plantain tree. A lady's dress, of the best kind of Piña cloth, will cost fifteen hundred dollars, and a Piña handkerchief will yield ten pounds.

It is admitted (*Athenæum,* number 1253) on all hands that the finest of the Dacca muslins exceed anything that can be produced by the looms of Europe. The tobes and sashes of Herar are hand-woven. They as far surpass (says a writer) in beauty and durability the vapid produce of European manufactories as the perfect hand of man excels the finest machinery.

No little skill in work and colours is shown in the Elk-skin coat, and the knife-sheath and belt, embroidered with moose-hair and porcupine quills and beads by the North American Indians, and no machinery of ours could make the fellow cloke to that of the King of the Sandwich Islands. Its ground is of matting, on which patterns are formed of rare and splendid feathers, "with a skill and grace worthy of the most civilized art." Its fabrication was carried on through eight kings' reigns, and it took the labour of a million dollars.

Mr. Shaw had seen rush baskets so closely woven by the Mission Indians as to be water-tight and to serve for buckets; and Hindoo cooks with few appliances, on a wild plain, would dish up a dinner that will allow little glory to our load of cooking gear.

There is another question of machinery, and it is its effect on the health of the workman's body or mind, or the reaction of machine work. If the reaction of labour with a machine is less bad than it is without it, then it is a good, and it is an evil whenever it may hold him in work of worse reaction. Agricultural machinery I think, on the whole, a physical good, as it takes off from hands some very heavy work of trying reaction, and holds the labourer in lighter toil. But there is machinery which holds the labourer in unwholesome places, and under unwholesome agencies, with too great a sameness of action and posture, and has to answer for a good share of torn limbs, broken bones, and untimely deaths, and of the evils already brought forth under the head of division of labour.

CONGREGATED LABOUR

STORED labour, in the form of capital and machinery tends to gather hand labour on one spot, and to form a body of congregated labourers, a state in which there may be both good and evil. The good of it is that all the labour is employed more readily under the oversight and direction of one ruling mind, and that the work can be easily transferred from one division of labour to another, and this is a good for the employer, while the evil of it is likely to be felt by the labourers and the people at large rather than the workers of capital.

Some of the evils of congregated labour may be, and often are, - I do not say always are or must be, - the well-known ones of scantiness of room, and of free air, and the thick herding of people in houses, with the consequences of sickness and impaired health of body and of mind. Where these evils, however, begin with the working classes they reach to others, for since by the laws of England, as well as the calls of Christian brotherhood, the men of lost health or spent labour are kept by the labour of others, so if capital were to increase itself by one-fiftieth by omitting to find healthy dwellings for its labourers, where it might build them, and therefore their health or working strength should be lost for a time or for life, it may happen that the overseer may call on capital for its fiftieth in the form of poors'-rates, and its own ultimate gain may be nothing; or else it would happen that the gain of the capital would be taken by the poors'-rate from other men who are taxed for its sick labourers.

Another case of congregated or machine labour is a needful and fair one, and yet one of which English freedom is not over fond, that it brings in a strict clock-service. A free-working razor-grinder may drive his treadle faster or slower, or stop his wheel at will, but a man bound to the tread-wheel cannot leave it nor slacken his steps till he has fulfilled his time; and so men who handle their own businesses, however small they may be, can work or play at will; whereas, in congregated labour in the hire of capital, minutes of labour become of more value to the employer as more hands are congregated on his work, and labourers are fairly bound to yield to a clock-service.

The truth is well stated in the following paper on Woolwich Arsenal:- "During the Crimean war, upwards of 10,000 men and boys were employed in the Arsenal. When such masses of men as this have to be dealt with daily, it is obvious how necessary it must be to possess an organized system by which the loss of what might otherwise be considered mere fractions of time, is noted. Let us suppose, for instance, that every man and boy in the Arsenal lost only five minutes per day, and it would amount in the aggregate to the loss of labour of one man for twelve weeks to the Government- *Woolwich Arsenal*." Thence it is clear how congregated labour will hold the workmen in clock-thraldom.

Another evil of congregated labour is that its throng of labourers are sometimes excited by sudden fits of crowd-moodiness to acts of violence, or a behaviour of defiance, and are the more threatening to the law of order and peace, as they are a greater throng; and thence the law, by reaction again, trenches on the freedom of the labourer by enactments against the conspiracy of strikes; and the tool-wielding hand must sometimes be holden to peace, if not to work, by the soldier's sword or policeman's bludgeon.

Another evil of congregated labour is one which, however, may appear in any fast increasing population, whether they may be drawn together in the service of one capital or of many; an outfalling from the ordinances of grace. The population under the care, for instance, of one sufficient church has at times increased so rapidly with the growth of a new branch of commerce, or the presence of a great working capital, that it has outgrown the accommodation of the place of worship, and the full outreaching of its ministration; and being collected from sundry places, have sunk into a godless and dark-minded form of life, before they have been bound into a Christian neighbourhood, or before the capital that has gathered them, or that their presence has increased, has taken for them that Christian care which our forefathers took in the endowing of churches for all collections of men. On this question light has been cast by the inquiry of a Committee of the House of Lords into the spiritual destitution of populous places.

As the increase of population increases the worth and income of land and houses, so where the new presence of a population has swollen the yearly rent of hundreds of pounds into thousands, it would not seem a hardship if the law should take a rated share of the people-bred rent for the ordinances of grace to the population that created it.

We can hardly believe that congregated labour can be overwhelmingly needful, since it is not found congregated in all lands in such cases as it holds with us. The cutting of the Bohemian glass is, I believe, carried on by men who work each in the quiet of his own house, which may be in the pretty nook of a village dell; and the carding and spinning of wool, and buttoning, were formerly home-work in this country.

SERVANTS

MUCH of the hand-service among the old nations was that of the slave or serf, born to thraldom, or brought into service under the sword of the invader; and his service was transferred from master to master, like that of a horse; not for wages, but for the price of man as a *living instrument,* which, indeed, is Aristotle's definition of a slave.

By the holy spirit of the Gospel, slavery has been unshackled in most Christian lands, and the free hireling has undertaken the work of the slave for wages. We have the poor always with us, and in communities of divided labour, and strong calls for mind work, there must be a need of hand-service.

But what is the true Christian view of servants, or of the service of one man's hands, that answer the hourly wants of another's body? It cannot be that in God's economy of the world servants are only to uphold the pleasure, or the pride of greatness, of their employers, for our Saviour shows us that the greatest in His kingdom is not he who has most hands waiting on him, while he works not for others; but he that does the greatest good service of mind or body for the happiness of others. "He that will be greatest among you, let him be your servant," for the Son of Man came not to be ministered unto, but to minister unto others.

The true Christian view of hand-service seems to be that servants are to be helpers in work, and to take lower work from their employers, and so to set their hands and minds free for work of higher kinds. The mind of King Alfred in the house of the herdsman, could ill perform the lower work of baking the cake, since he was busy with a far higher one, the deliverance of his people from the sword of the Danes, and therefore he needed for his own life-wants a service which the community could well afford to yield to him; and so the free time which is gained by the service of others in lower work is not afforded for idle pleasure, but for good work of a higher kind.

LABOUR REWARDED

IF we look at the usual rewards of work with a worldly rather than a godly mind, we may be greatly discouraged, since we shall see that callings or labours of least service to man's true welfare, are not unfrequently best rewarded by worldly gain. The keeping of a gin-palace or casino in a working population would be likely to win money faster than the preaching of temperance, or the keeping of a school for their children. An entertainment in juggling might gain more shillings than a lesson in knowledge; and a man has become richer as owner of a gambling-house than his neighbour by the letting of lodgings. The writing of a low novel may pay better than the publication of a book against a social evil.

The selling of one's conscience to powers of evil wins worldly rewards more readily than a standing by the truth against sin; and services to the rich, who do not need them, are a better investment for interest in gold than services to the poor, to whom they would be a blessing. With nations, a state wins more land and wealth by sending the sword against weak tribes than affording them missionaries or other good teachers; and we may be gaining money faster by selling the Chinese opium,- which is a bane to their health, - than we should by taking to them the most wholesome kinds of food.

In short, cunning and selfishness, and unrighteousness of several kinds, may bring in more ready money than goodness and truth; and while people freely honour the great man who can afford to keep a town-house, or a yacht, or a pack of hounds, or a carriage-and-four, or any costly luxury of the highest life, let us not withhold honour from the man who can afford to keep a conscience, which, if we reckon the worldly gain that must be foregone to hold that most precious treasure, is of the greatest cost.

If this small money reward of the servants of God happens under the providence of God, is He unrighteous? No: "Just and right is He." It only shows what He has told us in His word, of how little worth He holds money. A man may have one of two aims in his calling: (1) To get rich with a hope that he may work righteously; or (2) to work righteously with a hope of winning daily bread. The latter is the Christian mind, and the former is the decent worldly one.

It is sometimes said of the spending of labour in the form of money in folly, if not in vice, that it is good for trade, and it may be true, but what trade, good or bad? The true commercial use of capital is to spend it in labour, but I may spend capital on labour worthy of an angel, or the labour of demons. A landowner may bestow his capital on the improvement of his estate, and the houses, and sheds, and roads, and bridges of his people, or he may lay it out in a ship and tackle for the slave trade. In the former case it becomes at once an agency of good, and in the other it is an agency of evil; and so it either increases or diminishes the sum of happiness.

The prodigal son spent his substance in riotous living: good for trade, but evil for himself; and the true happiness of man, holiness; and, therefore, an angel over-watching the welfare of mankind would hardly be content with the answer that the spending of capital was good for trade, unless he knew whether it were a good or bad trade. I know it may be answered here that money spent in a brothel may pass through it to the baker, shoemaker, or other worldly craftsmen, and so work again immediately for good labours; and the money spent on the slave ship and crew and living freight may at once begin to win life-gear for labourers in England and Africa. True, God does not allow the capital which you may spend for bad labours to buy bad labours for ever. This would be to leave the whole world to sin, but yet there are labours of evil and of good to man; and although the commercial use of capital is to buy labour, the spending of it in bad rather than in good labour is not, *pro tanto,* good for trade. It is good for nothing.

LABOURS WITH GOOD REACTION

A QUESTION of great importance to man is, "What is the best labour for man's bodily health and welfare?" Though there is reason to believe that the most healthy modes of winning a livelihood were the earliest ones of hunting, herds-manship, and free tillage, in which there was a good action, without too long a toil, of the lungs and of all the limbs of the body in the open air. Although, in England, where hunting is a freely chosen sport, and not a needful toil for daily food, it is a pleasure for a prince; yet in Africa, where it is a needful work of most of the natives, it yields men little of the English hunter's joy, which the sold song says is in the chase, whereas the African's joy, although he must feel hunting to be a work of excitement, is in the ending of the chase, by a taking of a store of food.

Dr. Livingstone writes that some Africans seeing Englishmen hunting, said, "Have these hunters, who come so far and work so hard, no meat at home? Why these men are rich, and could slaughter oxen every day of their lives, and yet they come here and endure so much thirst for the sake of this dry meat." "Yes," answered the Englishman, "It is for the sake of play besides." This produces a laugh, as much as to say, "Ah! you know better," or "Your friends are fools."

Some savage or pastoral tribes of open-air life have become men of fine forms, graceful gait, and good action. Mr. Shaw writes of the men of the Navigator's Islands as the finest race of beings he ever beheld, for most of them were more than six feet high, and several walked up to him and rested their folded arms on his head. In Bhotan, Thibet, a traveller has written that the people are a very fine race, "scarcely any where else shall we find an equal proportion of men so straight and well made, and so athletic; many of them are more than six feet high, and deformity is almost unknown, except that from the goitre."

The Circassians are handsome and active men; and some tales of the good health and long life of the early Britons had reached the old Greeks and Romans, and they are not altogether unworthy of belief to those who have seen the teeth of old Britons who were buried in our barrows. They were all free of caries; but at the end of a full life were worn down. Yet that over-work is not good for the healthy comeliness of man, would seem to be shown by the Brahmins, who are not over-worked, and are the finest caste in India; and by the *works*, or nobles of the Circassians, who are the most high-minded and handsome class of the land.

The fetching of water from springs we deem well taken off our women's hands by wells, pumps, or waterworks, and yet the minds of many travellers have been charmed by the beauty and graceful gait of water-fetching girls in other lands.

Sir Woodbine Parish has told of the winning comeliness in figure and gait of the women at Parga, a village in Greece, where they fetch water on their heads from a spring a mile or more from home; and he found some of the finest men he had ever seen in a set of privileged porters, who carry goods on their heads, at a place near Genoa, in Italy. "Hindoo girls walk homewards," says Mr. Power, " with water to their vine-covered huts, their bodies swaying with *swanlike elegance,* as they walk with the brightly shining brazen vases poised on their heads;" and Dr. Layard writes, "That at the town of Samarrah, the women came to fetch their evening supplies of water, and gracefully bearing their pitchers on their heads, returned to the gates."

The statistics of the longevity, health, strength, and comeliness of sundry popula-tions and classes of men of sundry occupations, would not be a barren kind of knowledge, as it might lead to some happy counteraction of the evils of such labour as is of a bad physical reaction.

"Hassell's Tour of the Isle of Wight," printed in 1790, tells us, "There is not, per-haps, in the kingdom, a place where so many lovely girls attend the market as at Newport, and at the same time they are dressed with a degree of elegance far beyond what is usually observable in persons of their rank. The appearance of these charming girls not only excited our wonder and admiration, but we found that they attracted the envy of all the farmers' daughters in the neighbouring coasts." Whether there fair maids have transmitted their charms to the present blooming daughters of the island farms I know not, and it is a question the solu-tion of which may be perilous for a bachelor to undertake.

GARDENING

Among labours of good reaction, we may reckon gardening.

A SKETCH

I HAD been working in my garden. The sun was just below the horizon, and the dew was already on the smooth green walks, bordered by sweet-smelling roses and carnations. The stillness of the evening was broken only by the whistling of the blackbird, and the splashing of the water when the trout sprung after the lively insects that floated in wild mazes over the ponds. I sat down on a rude seat I had formed beneath some old trees, that darkened the twilight of the evening into gloom, and as the smell of the bean-blossoms was wafted along on the cool air, and I thought on the fruits and plants that were ripening around me, I exclaimed to myself, "O fortunatos, sua si bona nôrint, agricolas!" How happy, if they knew their bliss, are they who till the ground.

Gardening is one of the sweetest amusements that an unambitious man, who lives far from the din of cities can find; and it is so different from many pleasures which, besides being short, are followed by listlessness or remorse, that it gives one a long and pleasing anticipation of crops, and an increasing gratification while they are growing; and instead of being expensive, rewards a man for every hour he spends in it.

Gardening is an occupation pleasing in itself, because it gives one those cheerful feelings of high health, which always arise from exercise; and because one had always the pleasure of finding the plot, the path, or the border, visibly bettered by the shortest labour; and the growth of plants, the unfolding of blossoms, and the kerning of fruit, all our own, give us a lasting gratification, which is varied and increased as they assume their shapes and colours, in growing and ripening; and there is such a long succession of flowers and eatables, from the snowdrop that blooms and dies in the cold winds of February, to the gigantic rosemallow of August; and from the fair young potatoe, - the early fruit of the spring, - to the scarlet-blossomed stem of the late French bean; that the attention is never weary, and the appetite never cloyed.

But there are other gratifications in this pleasing occupation. For though the gardener knows that the smallest blade of grass is nothing less than a stupendous work of omnipotence, he yet finds that the growth of plants is regulated and perfected by his skill and attention; so that when he receives the fruits of the soil he has tilled, he proudly identifies his labour in the growth of them. And how much sweeter do things seem when they are the long-known productions of one's own soil, than when we buy them from strange hands! and how pleasing it is to know that whether one prefers the red and juicy radish, or the cucumber that stretches its rough and bulky body on the warm earth; or whether one wishes for the crooked pear, or the yellow apricot; all are within one's reach! and all one's own!

BENT OF MIND

BY the good ordinance of God, the minds of men are formed with various bents to sundry kinds of the world's work; so that there are always hearts, heads, and hands for all needful labours of the community, and so strong is often the bent of a man's mind, that whether under the name of a talent or genius, or a folly, it works in its mission amid the most hopeless circumstances, and against the most forbidding hindrances.

THE VILLAGE GENIUS.

(A SKETCH DRAWN MANY YEARS AGO FROM THE LIFE.)

IT is said that opportunity makes a thief: but without pretending to settle that matter, I am inclined to think that opportunity makes a great man; and that the thatch of a cottage shelters many a clever head which only wants an opportunity of bringing its faculties before the world to win its admiration, of which the following sketch, drawn from the life, may be considered a proof.

Erfinder was originally a brazier, but he has ingrafted so many different professions on the old stock, that I can no more tell you what he is now, than I can determine the colour of the chameleon: and to name the many branches he carries on, would be like roll-calling a regiment of militia. But to proceed to the main point of my story, Erfinder's head engenders inventions as fast as you can blow balloons out of a bowl of soap and water, and I believe one of his first was an improved hand-mill for the use of families living far from the miller, or whose grists might have been lightened by a too rigid exaction of toll. Not having influence enough in the world to set his mill going, he put it aside, and invented an instrument for drawing teeth, by a perpendicular force, without hurting the gum or jaw; and so many throbbing masticators have become the subjects of experiment by this instrument, that it is thought the tooth-ache is, for one generation, totally extirpated from the place; and if they were all healthy and in living jaws, nothing less than his mill would grind flour enough for them to work upon.

His brain next laboured for the defence of the person against robbers and burglars, and produced a curious air-gun, and a pistol with four barrels revolving round an axis, long before Colt had given his name to such an arm, and the experimental discharges of these new weapons against doors and the like about his house, have left them like a well-used target of a company of musqueteers.

He next made a pump that would yield the water "backstroke and forestroke," in a regular stream, instead of throwing it out at the alternate motions of the handle, like the old pumps; and for this invention he took a patent. We now lost him: he left the cheerful light of day, which had long shown us his lively face, and went down into the bowels of the earth, putting *up,* or rather putting *down,* his pump-work, and sending up the clear and wholesome water to the glad diarymaid and housewife.

He was at his old work of contriving as soon as ever he came above ground again; and having brought the air into his service by his air-gun, and got the mastery over the water by his pump, he determined that he would next attack fire; and for this purpose he invented an engine which would act as a pump in case of a leak in a ship, and as a fire-engine in case of fire. With the model of this engine he went to London, and the Lords of the Admiralty offered him leave to put one up in a ship for trial; but as he had a young family depending on his daily exertions at home, he could not afford the time or expense to do it, and he brought back his model and locked it up with the other neglected children of his brain.

I should need a volume to tell all his little contrivances: how he made a carriage to go by machinery; and fabricated horns, bugles, and flutes enough for a band of musicians; how he cut figures in bone, and invented instruments for drawing; and how, at the same time, he educated his own children with all the regularity of a pedagogue; and in this task he had pretty good materials to work upon, since his offspring are "chips of the old block." But after all, as Erfinder is settled in a village, and has not had an opportunity of bringing his abilities before the public, they have won him neither profit nor praise.

TRADES OVERSTOCKED

THAT crafts and callings may, at some times or places, be overfull one may believe, since at some times or places some callings may have shown themselves as very gainful, or have been felt of very good reaction to the mind or body, and so may have drawn too may men into them.

But the overstocking of all crafts or callings is not so common as has in some cases been conceived. If there is a population of 5000 people, with so many shoemakers as they need for their shoes, and then, with a sudden accession of people, more shoemakers were to settle beside the former ones, they may cry, but may cry without good grounds, that the craft of the shoemaker was overfull, though the lately-arrived shoemakers might be only those for whom there is a call in the feet-wants of the incoming population; and therefore the ratio of shoemakers to buyers of shoes might be the same in the increased population as it was in the unincreased one. So while in an increasing population in any land the ratios of the men in every calling to those of all others, are at first neither too great not too small, or are good ones, and then are preserved such, it is not at once very clear that any of their callings are overfull.

But it has been thought that all trades or handicrafts are overfilled, or that there are too many men at every kind of work, and spending their labour in the winning of life-gear which they are ready to give for the labour of others. Well then, if that were the case, every man could find men of every other calling ready to give him the life-gear of their labour for that of his own, and he may answer at least all his bodily needs, and would not feel his craft to be much overstocked.

If in a community there were land enough for their food, and there were enough of winners of food yielding food enough, then since the winners of food would be ready to buy other kinds of life-gear for their food, so yielders of life-gear would not necessarily feel the pinch of want; but if at any time through a want of food-winners the food of a community should fall short of their wants, then other businesses would at once be overfilled, since they would hold too many hands from the winning of food, which is the primary life-gear. *Venter magister artium*, and all craftsmen are in evil plight unless they can win food.

A calling may become overfilled with craftsmen from the increase of monopolies, or the uptaking of greater shares of the trade by men of capital. If farms are larger than they were a hundred years ago, they must have become fewer, and so the farmers' calling must have been found overstocked, unless some farmers had gone over to other callings. Now, the men who might so be shut out from the class of farmers would least disturb the ratio of food-winning labour, to labour that yields other kinds of life-gear, by undergoing - what might not be desired by themselves, or of good to others - the hardship of sinking into the class of hirelings, or by migrating to till the wild lands of colonies, whence we may draw food for other commodities; or by taking up the callings that work for agriculture, as that of makers of agricultural machines, or collectors or importers of manures, or searchers into agricultural chemistry; for since these callings are links in the chain of agricultural labours, of which the last but one is the farmer, and the last is his labourer, so if a man is outshut from work at the last link but one, and takes on work at another, he will still be, in a way, a winner of good, though by going into the series of other than food-winning labours he will increase the class of food consumers, and diminish that of food yielders.

Whether such changes as these may be an evil to the community will hinge on the ratios of labour in the sundry callings of life, within the whole circle of our outward and homeward trade in the whole world.

An Englishman writes of his going to Africa: "I was leaving England because I felt that I was *de trop* in a country where every profession was overstocked." This writer may mean that professions or callings of mind-work were overstocked; but it has been deemed that productive callings of tillage and handicrafts have been overstocked, as workmen have been strongly recommended to emigrate, and emigration societies have been formed to help them to other lands, and among them to Australia, where it was deemed that, owing to the great room for the primary craft of farming, other crafts were not overfull; but even in Australia, and even in food labours, crafts have been felt to be overstocked. An Australian writer in 1856 says, "Harvest was scarcely over when the ranks of the unemployed began to swell. Tired of seeking employment through the country in vain, labourers of all kinds are congregated in the towns, awaiting the commencement of public works, or any chance jobs which may arise."

Mr. Eburne, who wrote a book in furtherance of emigration to Newfoundland, in 1624, declares that in his time, when the population of England could not have been more than half of that of our days, all trades were overstocked. He writes:- "There bee so many of all trades, sciences, and occupations, that one cannot live for another. So it is with shopkeepers, they hardly can finde any place where to set up shop, all places being already full, and overfull:" so that if half the population of England were cast into the sea, trades would sill be overstocked.

If hardship in winning a livelihood is a token of an over-population, then the thinnest populations have been too dense. Some men found it hard to get a livelihood in the thin population of the Saxons. In Nicaragua (as Mr. Squier says), where not more than half of the clear lands is under cultivation, and among the few scattered Arabs of the basin of the plain of Shinar, men are found barely winning a livelihood; and there are insolvents in Australia. Here we are brought to the subject of over-population, of which we have no definition. If a twofold population can win food as fully as the single one in their place had gained theirs two generations before, then the greater population is no more an over-population than was the smaller one. We should distinguish between the living of a population *in* a place, and *on* a place. A population lives *in* the place of their abode, and *on* the land that yields them food. Now a blacksmith's household may be too many to win food on the space of his garden, but if he sells his labour to the farmers of his village, he lives *on* the land of the farms, and does not overburden them. So the people of a county town may be an over-population for the land of the borough *in* which they live, but not for the land of the county *on* which they may live; and so again, the people of Britain might be an over-population for the land of England if they lived *on* it, but are not so for the many lands in the world from which they can draw food, and *on* which they live by the out-sending and sale of their labour. There is no over-population until the people are too many for the land *on* which they live. The men of Tyre were not an over-population for their rock, while other lands (such as the king's country, - *Acts,* xii, 20) would give them food for their purple cloth, and other cunning workmanship; and there was no more need that they or the Venetians should leave their narrow abode, while they brought home food by traffic, than that a village blacksmith should go to the woods of Canada because his garden is not big enough to yield him meat and corn.

PAPER MONEY

IN a kind of day-dream which I had at the time of the money crisis, I saw two spirits, of whom one, *Look-a-head,* came and stood at my side, while the other, *Go-a-head,* was patting on the shoulder a specious swaggering fellow, and proclaiming his worth as a promoter of commerce. He had helped poor men into business, and had kept on the machinery of commerce with the timely oil of accommodation, where, otherwise, with the bare power of capital, it would have stopped. "Don't hearken to him," cried *Look-a-head.* "That fellow whom he is praising has lately shown himself one of the greatest rogues of the land; and under favour of the law - for the law often protects his delinquencies, where it would send the stealer of a turnip to jail - he has cheated hundreds and thousands of their little hoards of hard-earned savings, and left widows and orphans without bread; he is called *Paper Money."*

That paper money has been found useful is clear, or it would hardly have holden its place; but it is equally clear that the misuse of it has bred overwhelming evils to thousands of worthy people. I cannot conceive any other good reason in behalf of paper money than that it is a help to trade, and trade is rightly only a giving of labour in one form for labour in another; for the winning or giving of labour for nothing of labour is not trade, though, in one case, it may be tyranny, or begging, or cheating, or robbery; and in the other, generosity, or love, or bribery: and therefore all the paper money beyond that which represents and pledges the labour or life-gear under the hands of the givers of the paper pledge, is not a help to trade, but is a cheat, which is only likely to take from the holder of labour his life-gear for nothing, against which there is a curse, and a law that allows a man to cheat his neighbour as long as he can deceive him, is bad; and worse, if it punishes a small swindle and protects a great one.

If a cunning man wheedles money from a woman for a talisman which he makes her believe will keep her from the loss of a cow worth five pounds, when he knows his talisman is of no service, he is punished for obtaining money under false pretences; but if another cunning man wheedles wealth from her for a written talisman, which he makes her believe will secure her from the loss of her labour, worth a hundred pounds, though he knows that his talisman is of no service, as it pledges a nonentity, the law will most likely give him a certificate upon which he may go forth to sell other false, but legal, talismans of the same kind.

The law that protects men in the winning of others' labour, by the pledging of a nonentity for an actuality, is an evil rather than a good to trade. It may be answered that the bonds on which a state borrows the money of a national debt are a pledging of a nonentity, as it is a pledging of the labour of future years or generations; and yet that many deem a national debt a good. It may be a good to those who gain good by it, as slave dealing, or bribery, are of worldly good to those who thrive by it, but I think it is not a national good; and that the less we do in the pledging of nonentities for the call of our needs the better it is.

Let a man sell his cow and deliver her, but to sell his cow's next calf is not the fair trade of a thriving man; and to sell, for a stated price, the first forehead-starred calf that shall be born in lineal descent from his cow's first calf, is not trade but gambling. But in the sale of nonentities, there may be the nearest approach to fair traffic in the reckoning of the chances of their becoming actualities, and the rating of them at less worth upon the smaller chance. But men who take their neighbours' labour for a nonentity upon a bad promissory note, take the worth of an actuality by passing a nonentity off for one, and therefore a bad trade on false capital is worse than gambling.

The man who risks his neighbours' labour to win a gain by paper money will not give his neighbour a share of his gain if he wins, though if he loses his neighbour must bear the loss; and therefore his trade is, from the first, a most unfair and vicious one. But as his goods cost him little or nothing, he may sell them at lower rates than those of like goods for which their holders pay; so that they must lose money by business, or lose business, which is a hardship that the law ought to forbid, and buyers who gain by the lower prices of the unworthily-obtained goods, are themselves getting their neighbours' goods for nought; and no gain brings us a blessing unless it comes to us in the way of Providence as a legacy, or inheritance, or gift, or unless we receive it for some good, whether labour of body or mind, or concession of capital.

The name paper money, although I have used it is a false one; for paper so called, although it may be a pledge for money, is not so much money as all the odd wares in a pawnbroker's shop are money. Neither is it capital, for capital is stored labour, and a promissary note is a store of only the labour that brought to hand the sheet of paper with its writing; and, therefore, the greatest increase of paper-pledges for money is not the least increase of capital. It may be said, "Oh! if you forbid all paper money but that which pledges true capital, then you withhold men without capital from setting up large businesses." Be it so. Great capital and great businesses are, in the usual order of Providence, the reward of long labour, and care, and uprightness; and if a man, without the use of these good seeds of wealth, is yet to have their fruits, let his friends give him his capital and business, but let him not tax his neighbours to raise himself to the level of the long-worn son of toil. To find men shorter ways than industry to sufficiency, is not the way to promote industry.

SELLING AND BUYING

SELLING is the giving of labour of one form for labour in another, though it means now the giving of labour in any form for money. *Sellan* or *syllan* meant formerly to *give* or *hand over* for an equivalent or not; and the words "Give us this day," in the Lord's Prayer, in Saxon, are "Syle us to-daeg," though now to *sell* is to give for money.

An early form of sale and purchase is that of the dumb barter of seekers of the raw wealth of men of unknown speech, in which goods may be placed on the shore by one of the peoples, and the others may place beside them such a lot of their own as they wish the others to take for them; and so after much higgling, by upcomings and withdrawings, or increased biddings in the form of other goods, a bargain is made. However rude may seem this form of trade, it is to be feared it had been chosen in our land by receivers of stolen plate, in cases in which biddings are offered for it in money placed before the thief by an unseen buyer.

Although the first form of traffic, or of the exchange of labour in the form of life-gear, was barter, or the giving of one kind of life-gear for another, this form of trade was after a while shortened by the taking what has, at last, assumed the form of money, or some one commodity which might be taken as a rating standard of other commodities, whether it were a cow, or a sheep, or aught else. So Mr. Drayson says of the African Kafirs:- "The Kafir notation is different from ours, they calculate so many elephants' tusks, so much money; so much money, one cow; six cows, one wife, this being the highest currency among them."

Higglings for animals and other goods of unsettled price, are sometimes funny to a bystander, from the difference of the buyer's and seller's prices, and the skill with which each tries, by cautious approaches to his neighbour's prices, to bring them by more rapid transitions to a meeting with his own.

A market is in Saxon *an ceap*, our word *cheap*, which means bargain, and to buy a thing *cheap,* or *cheaper,* was to buy it good *cheap* or better *cheap*, good or better bargain, like the French *bon marché.* From cheap, a market comes Chippenham, Chipping Norton, *Chepstow, Cheapside,* and *East Cheap.*

The holding of a fair was a privilege bestowed on a place by royal grant, and in former times of rarer shopstores, they were as handy for housekeepers as they were gainful to landowners, since body-gear and house-wares, that are now in shops of every town and village, were borne on strings of pack-horses from fair to fair, where housekeepers laid in a half-year's or a year's supplies, as they often did even of beef for the winter board. By the laws of Edward and Athelstan, no one was to buy outside the gate of the market or fair town, without a witness, the portreeve, or some other true man.

Selling goods by sample or specimen is very handy among men of good faith, for the sparing of the labour of carrying great weights, but bad faith has too often been known to affect sales on samples better than the bulk, or to send in a bulk of worse quality than the sample. The Greek *facetiæ* afford a funny joke of sale by sample, as that of an idle fellow who had a house for sale, and went to market with a stone drawn out of the wall as a sample of it.

Sale of goods by auction, or increasing biddings, is a very early form of sale, as it was one of those among the Romans. Some of their writings speak of it, and the word *auctio,* an increasing, bespeaks the increase of the biddings. It is said of a Roman, Hortensius, as a token of his wonderfully retentive memory, that he sat all day at an auction, and in the evening could tell the goods, prices, and order, and buyers of all the lots. Auctions among the Romans were announced by bill, tabula, or crier, and some think from a passage in Cicero *De Off,* 223, and of Lucian in his "Sale of the Philosophers," that the crier put up and recommended the lots at the sale. It was as usual to make the best of goods by hand-touches and praises among the Greeks and Romans as it is with us. Lucian makes Jupiter say at the sale of the philosophers, "Place the men in order, but first adorn them, that they may look handsome, and draw bidders." And when Mercury asks Jupiter if he shall put up Diogenes, he calls him "that dirty fellow of Pontus," but when he puts him up, he cries, "I now put up a noble lot (life), and excellent, generous, and free man."

The auction would seem a fair form of sale for the winning of the best prices for the seller, without wrong to the buyer, but this again is often vitiated by bodies of confederates, whether brokers or others, who worry free bidders by offensive opposition, and then divide the goods among themselves by a sale called a "knock out," and thus more than make up the individual losses of their collective opposition to the sellers by their collective gains of it.

AUCTIONS, A SKETCH

"Na almoeda tem a barba queda." - PORTUGUESE PROVERB.
"At a sale keep your beard still."

WHAT a seducing thing to the idle is a sale in a village! how gratifying to guess our neighbour's plan in bidding for this or that article; to discover what young woman is near matrimony, from her buying "something towards housekeeping;" how pleasant to hear the witty sayings of the auctioneer, that one may relate them to one's next tea party; and above all, to sit in continual expectation that fortune may throw a "good bargain" into our hands.

To vary the quiet sameness of a village existence, I lately went to one of these animated scenes, where I found that the auctioneer's jest and jug had put the company into so good a humour, that the wise admonition of my proverb seemed quite disregarded. Another proverb - a good comment on mine - says, "What we do not want, is dear at any price;" and believing in the truth of the assertion, I could not help smiling at some of my neighbours' "good bargains." The roasting-jack was knocked down to a poor widow, with whom it was likely to make as many revolutions in a year as the earth does; a cradle became the property of a patriarch whose offspring had reached the height of the military standard; and half-a-dozen chairs "went off" to a recruiting sergeant. In one part of the room the matron was examining her china; in another, the damsel inspected her chest of drawers, blushing with the idea of depositing in it, ere long, her wedding dress, and other acquisitions of her industry and expected prosperity; while a wicked little girl behind was pinning the village schoolmaster's black coat (in which he had ruled two generations of scholars) to the blacksmith's fustian jacket.

When the last lot had been knocked down, I went home, and sitting down by the fire-side, fell into the following train of thought. - How different are the circumstances in which men expose their property to public sale: sometimes the individual is about to "change his residence;" then his mind is busy with the thoughts of a fresh habitation, new connexions, and different occupations, and he is delighted with the foretaste of prosperity, or agitated by the fear of a reverse. Sometimes he is "retiring from business;" then he is happy in the hope of leaving the bustle of the world and gliding through a smoother existence; he fore-enjoys the genteel cottage in the pretty village, the morning drive in the neat little vehicle, the arm-chair by the fireside, and the snug tea-party of kind neighbours. Sometimes his goods are seized by the sheriff for rent. Alas! a sale is generally followed by a change of circumstances, and that is a thing which, at best, fills the mind with solicitude; but the feelings of an honest man in the last case are horrible. The thought of coming poverty makes him sad, the necessary dispersion of his children chills his heart, he trembles with agony when he thinks of the sorrows and sufferings of his wife, and the villany of men who have cheated and deserted him, almost excites him to madness; but he reflects on the former goodness of God and remembers his own sins, and weeps.

A sale of the last-mentioned kind of an uncle's stock, and which I saw when a boy, made on my mind a strong impression. My uncle was a farmer in the West of England, but became insolvent from the depression of the agricultural interest after the end of the French war. My aunt had a numerous family, and her long exercised solicitude as a mother, and her continual struggles against misfortunes, had nearly brought her with sorrow to the grave; she was calm, and it was only when either of her daughters passed her, that a tear rolled down her sallow cheek. The young men were in that severe and reckless mood in which men are frequently thrown when assailed by misfortunes which they can still resist. The girls were bewildered, and scarcely knew what happened around them; then were driven away the cows under which the weeping milkmaid had so often sung the simple songs of the country; then went the waggon in which the merry haymakers had so many times ridden in to the feast of a harvest-home; and in short, then everything that was dear from familiarity was taken away, and my uncle, as he looked on the fields he had so long cultivated with hope, and of which he had taken the produce in grateful joy, sighed and dropped a tear as if he had said "Dulcia linquimus arva."

The sale or the buying of a brother man, or a slave, demoralises the trader in life, and makes him unfaithful to manhood itself. When men buy and sell others, as cattle, they yearn to believe, for the peace of their conscience, that they are below the humanity of their own blood. Americans have been heard to call their slaves "black cattle;" and the Portuguese, in Angola, call a slave *o diabo*, the devil; *o bruto*, the brute; *o bicho*, the grub. And when Lucian makes Mercury to sell, as slaves were sold, the Greek philosophers, he does not call them men, but *lives*. "You," says Jupiter, "put up the lives," *steeson toos veeoos;* and then he cries, "I offer an excellent life," *ariston veeon polo*. To bestow *wrongfully* a bad name on another is to bring a reaction of harm on our own minds.

The selling of goods by raffle or lottery is not of good effect on the mind of the winner, since he gains the unwillingly-lost labour of his fellow tryers, and he is, so far, led to trust for his goods to chance rather than to labour; and the very name *raffle*, meant, in old English, *plunder* or *spoil;* as if the winning was that of plunder or spoil taken from the unwinners.

For the sake of fair traffic, men have chosen sundry forms of selling commodities, as to quantity by head or tale, or by weight and measure; and as to form of sale by hand, by standing price, by auction, by contract, or by lottery. Selling by tale is by the head or by number, and often by lots, or set numbers, as by the couple or brace, as fowls; by the dozen or gross as eggs, quills or pens; by the score or by the hundred, as bricks or teazles. Sale by tale is fair, so long as the same tale contains the same quantity of like quality, and the quantity is such that the reckoning is of less labour than the measuring or weighing. The payment of a tax by head, however, in the old poll tax, was felt to be so wrong, that the call for it bred an insurrection under the smith, Wat Tyler.

Measuring and weighing are fair so long as the measures and weights are true; but, unhappily, the scant measure and the uneven beam, and the bag of deceitful weights, which were an abomination to God among the Jews, are still so much to be feared with us, that inspectors are sent forth to try them. The standard yard measure for England (which is of brass, marked with two golden studs), and the standard pound, are kept by the Clerk of the House of Commons. But as metal varies in bulk by heat and cold, and both the standard yard and pound may be lost or broken, so an Act of the 1st of May, 1825, declares that the brass yard shall be a standard only at the temperature of 62° Fahrenheit, or that a yard is 36 parts out of 39.1393 parts of the length of a pendulum that swings seconds in a vacuum, at the sea level, in the latitude of London; and that a pound weight shall be a certain quantity more than 22 times the weight of a cubic inch of rain water, weighed in air by brass weights, at the temperature of 62° Fahrenheit.

The insufficiency of weight alone, and the help afforded to it by measure, are shown by the use which was first made of specific gravity by Archimedes. King Hiero had weighed out to a goldsmith some gold to make a crown, and though his crown came back of the true weight of his gold, he thought the goldsmith had kept some of it, and made up the weight by an alloy, and he sent the crown to Archimedes that he might try it. After much idle thought it struck the mind of Archimedes, as he went into the bath, and saw the water rise by the immersion of his body, that a weight of coarse metal would be bigger, and would displace more water, than a like weight of a finer metal, and thence that a crown of base alloy would displace more water than its weight in pure gold; and so, on perceiving a way of trying the impurity of the crown, he ran out crying *Eureeka,* "I have found it," and thence we have the use of specific gravity.

A person is sometimes asked in joke, which is the heaviest, a pound of lead or a pound of feathers, and his querist laughs at him if he answers that one is heavier than the other, though the laugh may be fairly turned against the querist if he says they are of equal weight, since a pound of feathers, as they are weighed in air, would outweigh the pound weight in a vacuum. A pound of feathers must displace more air than a pound of lead in falling, and therefore must be overloaded against the smaller lump of lead, and in a vacuum the overloading feathers would soon become overweight.

A corn of barley was formerly made a standard in long measure, and three of them were found or made an inch, and a grain of wheat was made a standard weight, of which twenty-four were the weight of a silver penny, or pennyweight. The weight of a silver penny was a standard weight of which twenty made an ounce. And *Asser* says that King Alfred caused as much wax as could equal the weight of seventy-two pennies, to be made into six candles for chronometers, as well as lights.

Henry I ordained that the ell *(ulna)* should be the length of his own arm, and his standard measure was confirmed by Henry III in 1257, and again under Henry VII in 1492.

Most of our measures were at first taken from limbs of the body, as a *foot,* a *palm,* a *hand,* in the height of horses; a *yard,* the *geard* or *gyrd* or girth of a man's body; an *ell, elne,* the *ulna,* or lower arm-bone. A *cubit,* the length of the lower arm-bone, in Latin *cubitus,* the leaning bone on which a man leans sideways; a *span,* the *pace* or *step,* a *nail,* and a *fathom,* the embrace, or length taken in by the clasping of arms.

The truest measure will not bind a rogue to fairness, as was shown by the bad faith of Quintus Labeo, who made peace with King Antiochus on condition that he should have half of his fleet; on which he cut all of his ships in two, and took a half of the halves, leaving the king without a single ship.

Some of the names of our solid measures are of rather curious etymology. A *firkin* was a *fourken* or a little *fourer*, as four of them make a barrel; a *kilderkin*, as appears by the Dutch *kinderkin,* is a *cildercin,* a child or baby barrel; a *pottle* is a diminutive of *pot,* or name for such a pot as a pannier, under the expression a horse and pots; or as the wicker shield in cudgels was called the *pot,* and the peck was a *pocca,* or *poke,* which was a kind of bag, from which we have "to buy a pig in a poke," and the diminutive *pocket.*

The names of some measures answering, among the measures of some other peoples, to our yard, seem to have been taken from the length of a man's staff, as the Italian *canna,* or *cane,* and the Welsh *llath,* a staff.
Payment for work by toll, or a set share of the goods on which labour was bestowed, was in former times not unusual, nor, in itself, unfair mode of payment. Toll was often the wages of the miller for grinding; and by the laws of Ina, the King of Wessex, a man that took in his neighbour's pigs to fatten on the mast of his wood, was paid by a toll of the same. Of those fattened to three fingers deep, he took every third; for fat of two inches deep, every fourth; for a thumb's breadth, every fifth.

The system of truck, in which the employer of labourers keeps a store of commodities, of which, by circumstantial tyranny, he compels them to buy for their life-gear at prices and qualities of his choice, is a pernicious form of the tyranny of capital.

In some cases the laws have holden goods at given prices, though in different cases they were priced for different ends. With the Saxons and old Cymry commodities were priced for the sake of justice, so that the stealer or spoiler of them, or his fellow tithing-men or tribesmen, might be called, on fair grounds of warning, to make compensation to the owner; but in later times, some kinds of life-gear, such as bread, was priced against extortion, by a law-rating called an assize. The assize of bread was known to our law from the time of Henry III, 1266, down to that of

William IV. Though it might formerly have been of some good service, yet, as the commercial value of meal is shifting, it may have done as much wrong to sellers as it off-warded from buyers, and it is now abolished. Paying for services by usual and yet undefined fees, whether drink money or bakshish, although it may have begun in generosity, tends to become inveterate and heavy, as well as annoying, exactions.

Cicero *De Officiis* treats of the question of good faith in the sale of goods. He proposes a question that a good man has a house for sale, but he knows that it is unhealthy, and so badly built of bad materials, that in a little time it will fall. Ought he or ought he not to tell a buyer the bad truth, which is not or cannot be known to him? Anipater held that he ought not to conceal it, and Diogenes Babylonius that he is not called on to tell it. Antipater, a heathen, held that the concealing of the truth was as bad as the not showing to an off-wandering man his missed road, which, with the Athenians, was a hateful crime; and Cicero takes it, not as the act of a fair, upright, and good man, but that of a sly, cunning, and bad one. It is hardly allowed by the golden law of Christ, "to do to others as we would others should do to us."

Another case put by Cicero is that of a man who has freighted wheat to a shore where there is famine, and knows what is unknown to his buyers, that others ships of corn are a little behind his own. Ought he to tell them that fact, or to conceal it for the sake of getting a higher price for his own corn? Antipater held that he should tell the truth, and Diogenes Babylonius thought he might fairly conceal it. The seller of a slave was bound by the edict of the *ediles curules* to declare any defect. So that the Romans could see the wrong of cheating a buyer of his money, but not that of robbing a slave of his freedom, which he never sought to sell.

Another case put by Cicero, is that of a man *Pythius,* who had a garden and lodge by the shore, at Syracuse; Canius, a Roman knight, wished to buy it, but Pythius made him understand that he did not wish to sell it, though he would let it to him, and invited him to dinner on another day, and then hired fishermen to be fishing with fish in their boats, in the water before his lodge, and to bring him fish as if they had been caught within his fishing-right, so that Canius was led to believe the place conferred the right of fishing in water full of fish, of which it had none, and was cheated into the buying of it at a high price.

As the best of the heathen Greeks and Romans could not justify such a case of bad faith, or smartness as we may call it, we can take but little honour as Christians from the adulterations of our improved preparations for the stomach. The *Lancet,* in 1851, revealed great adulteration of food, such as mustard with flour and turmeric, coffee with chicory adulterated with something less good, bread with alum, and so with too much water, tea with Prussian blue, turmeric, blacklead, gum, sulphate of iron, and leaves of other plants than tea; and lately we have heard of the deaths of many people in a course of circumstances beginning with the use of *daff* instead of flour.

IMPROVEMENTS

I CONFESS I do not myself hail all the changes which come in under the name of improvements, with the cry, "Come in, good angel, you are wholly welcome!" I am more inclined to say, "Yes, come in, and let us try you," or "Come in if you are alone; but many of your name are followed by a demon that brings us a set-off of evil almost equal to your good."

I believe that most of our so-called improvements either displace a good, or bring in their train some evil, and that our true progress in well-being is only the difference of good between the good of the so-called improvement, and the good displaced by it, or the evil which follows it. As instances of what I mean, there was formerly made in boots an improvement of revolving heels, or heels that, as they wore down at the hinder edge, might be turned on a pivot, so as to bring the unworn edge into the harder wear, that they might last the longer; but the pivot soon became loose, and the heel slipped round, and threw the wearer on his back, with his coat in the dirt, and very likely his elbow on a flint, or his backhead on a flagstone; and so, on rating the gain of the improvement as reckoned in shoe leather, with the bad reaction of dirty coats, broken skin, if not bones, and small medical bills; the balance of good was nothing, and the improvement was given up.

The waterproof mackintosh was an improvement on open cloth; but as in action it confines the body-steam, - which, upon a man's resting from action, condenses to the wetting of his linen, and chilling of the body under it, - so the balance of good with the waterproof cloth is not always barely the being kept dry, instead of becoming wet through; but sometimes only the difference of being wetted through the coat, with rather free evaporation, and wetted under it with condensed body-steam.

So some man has devised an improved method of killing ticks, lice, &c., in sheep, by a chemical solution; but it seems that in a case given by the newspapers, a great evil is behind it. "Mr. Bird, farmer, at Burton, near Bamburgh, in Northumberland, had a flock of 867 sheep, which were recently 'dipped' in the chemical solution, and then turned out to grass. It is supposed that this solution was washed off the sheep by a shower of rain, and fell upon the grass, which being eaten by the sheep, poisoned them, as they began to die on the 16th instant, and on the 21st instant, only 26 out of the flock of 867 remained alive."

Our forefathers sometimes rode home from the merry boards of their friends following two lamps, called moons, fastened on the feet of a man on horseback, who rode on to pick out the road before them; and afterwards the lamps - I beg their pardon, the moons - were by an improvement grounded on another, taken from John Stridesaddle's boots, and fastened on the carriage, so that the outrider's labour was saved. The gain of good by carriage lamps is not barely light instead of darkness, but the difference of the two clear quantities of good afforded by the two forms of lighting the way. It may be said that there is a clear gain in money on the side of the carriage lamps, as they free us from the cost of the outrider; but no: whereas are forefathers spent money on the moon-booted outrider, on a bad and uncostly road, we spend it on the making of a better and more costly road; and our gain in money is the difference between the cost of the labour of John and his horse, and that of our good road over John's track.

I fancied, in a kind of day dream, that I had before me two spirits, one *Go-a-head,* who was praising all so-called improvements as all good; and another, *Look-a-head,* who was whispering to me that the so-called improvements were mostly forms of mixed good, and showing me their off-sets of evils. *Go-a-head* was boasting of a chest of drawers and a mattress, which were offered at half the usual price of such goods. "No," said *Look-a-head,* "not such ones; the drawers are not dovetailed, but clung together with glue, and the cotton mattress holds a lot of moss or hay inside of a film of cotton." Then *Go-a-head* was showing up a frock stuff, at a price which, he said, showed the blessing of machinery. "Nay," whispered *Look-a-head,* "don't you see the girl crying and the old woman laughing out yonder?" The girl had made a frock of the cheap stuff, and on stooping, like a good girl as she was, to pick up a pin, it had split all down her back, and the old woman who is laughing at the flimsy frock, is a Welsh woman, who gives half-a-crown a yard for hand-woven gown-stuff that wears like leather." *Go-a-head* praised some bleaching fluid, by which yarn was bleached in far shorter time than that of field-bleaching; but *Look-a-head* whispered, "If you want strong holland buy brown holland. His bleaching fluid rottens the fibre of the flax; it has also killed all the fish of his length of stream, and the fruit trees of his garden." *Go-a-head* pulled out of his pocket a paper, which he praised as a contract for building a church, and a great improvement on the loose understandings on which builders wrought in the old times under bishop architects. "Ah!" cried *Look-a-head,* ask him how it happened that the tower of a lately-built church fell down before it was fully up, and whether he will show you the long bill of side-charges that is hanging out of his pocket, with the law-papers which have been called forth by a lawsuit on a breach of contract?"

You see that shepherd yonder looking so sad. His sheep are dying on turnips. Neither man nor quadruped can live on, in good health, on one species of plant; and the Allwise had afforded sheep on the down twenty species, even of grass, and twenty or thirty species of other plants . *Go-a-head* has, however, recommended all the natural sward to be taken up, so as to rear, as food for the sheep, only turnips, or at most, two or three species of plants. He was showing up some improved stall-fed beef; but an old housewife, who had tried it, shook her head at it, and called it a lump if oily stuff which, under the trial of boiling and consumption was beaten by the graziers' beef of the rich open meadow. *Go-a-head* was praising the improvements in dyeing on a large scale, but *Look-a-head* showed me some dyers, and not very sweet-aired dyers, whose stained faces and hands were less comely than those of a tattooed savage, and their work far less healthy than the hunting of the uncivilized son of the bush. *Go-a-head* praised the division of labour which yielded the dresses in which were shown the charms of a company of young ladies, and wished to compare them with the gear of women of lower civilization, in which each daughter of Eve is her own dressmaker. "Can he tell us," answered *Look-a-head,* "how many fair girls and needle-women are worn into decline and slowly killed by over-confinement, and the overwork of the divided labour?" *Go-a-head* was praising a gentleman who has thrown several small farms into one, and let it to a wealthy and intelligent tenant, with capital enough to buy it, and therefore to work it effectually with the best machinery. "Look," said *Look-a-head,* "at those loads of old oak house-goods, and those moody men with their weeping wives and daughters: they are the tenants of the small farms, going adrift on the world, where land is now to be let to money, and not to labour. The labourers, driven off the land, have crowded in the close gardenless houses, and breed fever of which they are dying; and those careworn men at their doors are the tradesmen of the place, who are hopeless of food or health, through the rate-gatherer and fever.

"The farmers in China, as a class, are highly respectable, but as their farms are all small, they are probably less wealthy than our farmers in England. Each farm-house is a little colony consisting of three generations, namely, the grandfather, his children, and his children's children. There they live in peace and harmony together, all who are able to work on the farm, and if more labour is required, the stranger is hired to assist them. They live well, dress plainly, and are industrious, without being in any way oppressed. I doubt if there is a happier race anywhere than the Chinese farmers. The natives of Nantsin seem well to do in the world, having plenty of work without oppression, and enough to procure the necessaries and simple luxuries of life: like bees in a hive each contributes his portion to swell the general store. And so it is with almost every production in the celestial empire." - *Fortune's China.*

"The farmers of farmlings, or little plantations, having no labour, but working on the small patch on which they were born and have an affection for, are certain to expend far more labour on their own land, and to bring it to a much higher degree of cultivation than it would suit the purpose of a large planter to do, who, like the Australian or Canadian colonist, would probably find it more for his interest to cultivate a large surface imperfectly." - *McMicking's Recollections of Manilla, &c.*

Go-a-head was admiring a man who had attained the acme of enjoyment in highly civilized life, the pursuit of hunting and a yacht. "Oh!" said *Look-a-head*, "one of our voyagers knew an Esquimaux who hunted freely from Point Barrow to Jones's Island; and another voyager to the Marianne Islands found the men each with a proa of his own."

"Many years ago an attempt was made to discountenance the growth of chestnuts, by prohibiting their plantation in soils capable of other kinds of cultivation; but shortly afterwards the decree was revoked, on the report of no less a political economist than the celebrated Turgot. Vicent donc ces châtigniers magnifiques, quand méme! And may the Corsicans learn not to abuse the gifts which Providence gratuitously showers from their spreading boughs. It seems almost incredible that any man, even a political economist, should be guilty of such absurdity and such wickedness as to grudge the poor a food which they can obtain easily and in abundance. Which is the first requisite for mental improvement? Leisure - the being able to live without manual labour. But because the chestnuts conferred this inestimable blessing of leisure upon a class which, according to political economists, have no business to think, down were to come the chestnut trees. In their place the philosophers would have had mines and factories, in which Corsican men, women, and children should be subjected to labours which would degrade their bodies and minds, while the blessing of leisure should be confined to a few capitalists, whose business it should be to govern the said degraded men, women, and children." - *Literary Gazette,* June 12, 1858.

No wealth can make all men so rich that none shall be again called to labour. "The poor ye have always with you." However tall a man is, and however high may be his head above the dirt of the ground, some part of him, his feet, must be down on it; and the higher his face may be, the greater may be the weight that his feet have to uphold. So, the more may be the unworking men, who yield no service of hand or mind to the community, the worse is the task of the burdened workers; and therefore in a community of many rich idlers, care should be taken of the honest working classes, or else they will become degraded and dangerous.

TAXATION AND LABOUR

IT has been said that a small national debt is a national good; but as long as ours is compared with those hitherto owned by other nations, or that to which England was pledged before Pitt's time, and not with what it may unhappily hereafter become, it will not have the pretty quality of smallness to recommend it to the minds of taxpayers. It has been believed, for I have heard the belief of it uttered, that even a great national debt is a great good, inasmuch as it is an extension of the small one, which is a good; and inasmuch as it affords more people a living or a settled income from their hoarded and otherwise unproductive gold. This argument, however, would hold to be a blessing a national debt increased to a weight which the productive classes could not possibly bear, and which must wreck the social constitution of the nation, and that would surely be an evil; and therefore as such an argument would hold an undeniable evil to be a good, it cannot be a sound one.

A national debt is a good thing to those who have the good of it; and those are not the owners of the toilworn hands that produce the wealth whereby it is to be paid.

We knew, a few months ago, of a band of musicians, who, in steering of a dark night all in a row from a mansion, missed the path, and the leader of them was tripped headlong, to the great peril of his vocal shell, over some obstacle on the lawn. "That's lucky," cried "il secondo." "What do you mean by that?" answered the fallen son of Apollo, "con molto fuoco." "I meant," replied his friend, "it was lucky that I was not the foremost so as to get that fall."

In saying this much of the national debt, I am so far from imputing any the least blame to fundholders, that I should not be at all sorry to find everybody in England made my debtor to-morrow. But though I might be so selfish as to rejoice that the succession of a manor had been unfairly diverted from another to me, it would not make the diversion more desirable to the heir of the land; and if the increase or the greatness of the national debt be an evil to the nation as a nation, our legislators should do their best to withhold it from increasing, and to lessen it.

The population of England and Wales in 1841, was 16,035,797.

In the Army were about	37,603 persons.
In the Navy	40,000 Persons
Professional Persons	53,475 "
Miscellaneous Unproductive Persons . .	124,737 "
In the Government Civil Service	14,182 "
Officers	22,190 "
Independent Persons	453,149 "
In Almshouses, Prisons, &c.	177,379 "
Making	922,715 "
Servants to Independent and Professional Persons (one to five) would be about . . .	110.000 persons
In all about	1,032,715 "
Then the whole population lessened by the unproductive classes or	16,035,797 persons
	1,032,715 "
Will be.	15,003,082 "

But of these many are children and old folk, and therefore unproductive. Let us see how many of these are children under 10 years old. There are born yearly 3,197 children to 10,000 inhabitants: and therefore, by the solution of a proportion, we shall find there will be born yearly to 15 millions, 479,550, which being multipled by..10, will produce 4,795,500 for the children born to the 15 millions in ten years.

All these, however, will not be alive at the end of ten years; and therefore they are not to be taken as the actual number of children under ten among the 15 millions. Now by the census of 1841, the children under five years old were 1,323 of every 10,000 inhabitants, which would give 1,984,500 out of 15 millions of souls. The census tables do not give any expression for children under ten years old, but we can derive one, that will not be very wide of the truth, from the Carlisle tables. The census tables give as the yearly births 479,550, which will be 2,397,750 in five years. And the Carlisle tables give 47,309 children living at the end of five years, out of every 50,000 born in the five years; and this fraction $47309/50000$ of the 2,397,750 born in five years, would give about 2,268,700, a little more than two millions of children alive under five years old. The census gives a little less than two millions; and therefore only shows that our deductions from the Carlisle tables are not wide of the truth, and consequently may be taken as a trustworthy mode of calculation.

Now if there are 479,550 born in one year, there are ten times as many, or 4,795,500 born in ten years; and the Carlisle tables give about 80,000 as living at the end of ten years, out of every 100,000 born in the ten years; and this fraction $80000/100000$ or $8/10$ of the 4,795,500, will give 3,836,400 children under ten years old, and therefore, as we may suppose, unproductive, among the 15 millions of the productive classes in England and Wales.

But the fractional expression for the children of the unproductive classes in England and Wales will be true for those of Scotland or of the whole of Great Britain, 27 millions of souls.

Now $1032715/16035797$ the ratio of the unproductive to the productive classes may be taken in round numbers as $1/16$; and $1/16$ of $27m/1 = 27/16$ 1,685,000 of unproductive persons in Great Britain. Then 27,000,000 - 1,685,000 = 25,315,000 of the productive classes. Then from the expression for the children of the 15 millions under ten years old, we can get the number of children under ten years among the 25,315,000. They will be $= 38364/150 \times 25315/1 = 6,474,564$, or about 6,474,000 children under ten years old in Great Britain.

From the Carlisle tables we can draw, by a like calculation, an expression for individuals above 80 years old, and unproductive from infirmity. It is $7/2000$; and $7/2000$ of $25315000/1 =$ about 88,600 old folk above 80 years old, and therefore unproductive from infirmity. Then we have

```
Unproductive persons . . . . . . 1,685,000
Children under ten years . . . . . 6,474,000
Old folk above 80 years . . . . .     88,600

    Unproductive persons . . . 8,247,600
```

In addition to these we may reckon for those who are out of work through sickness, and unproductive as girls above ten years old, and weakly women; and they would make the unproductive about 8 1/2 millions or 9 millions of souls; and 9 millions from 27 millions, would leave 18 millions of hands to produce the national income.

Now the interest of the National Debt is 28 millions of pounds, which is to be produced by 18 millions of persons and $28/18 = £14/9$ each. Then reckoning that a labourer's work earns him 10s. a week, or £26. a year, or that he works 10 hours a day for £26. a year, we have as £26. : 10s. : : $14/9$: x

$$\text{or } 26 x = 140/9$$
$$\text{or } \quad x = 140/234 \text{ hours.}$$

Where x is the daily time in hours, which he has to work to make up his share of the money owing yearly to the fund-holder; and it comes out of ·6 of an hour or 36 minutes.

The interest of the National Debt therefore imposes upon the hands of the productive man, every day, 36 minutes of labour over that which he is bound to do for all other calls, whether those of his own body, or of his children, or of the poor's rates, or municipal, or other public objects; and the whole taxation of 50 millions, calls upon him for more than an hour's daily labour.

But our deductions of unproductive hands are not great enough; for very few work till they reach their eightieth year, and the production of the nation's income lies heavier on some classes than on others; and thence arise the stern calls for a lengthening of the daily labour of the toilworn body, which so often leaves a man no evenings wherein his mind may wander free, while his body may rest on the bench by the cottage door, or by the hearth amid the gambols of his smiling children; and which leaves him no time to strengthen the bonds of the hallowed love of kindred; no time to solace himself with the gifts of God, the *"domus et placens uxor;"* no time to enlighten and purify his soul by a peaceful reading of the Word of Life; we were going to say no time for the ordinances of grace, for too often the overworked body, if it has the rest of a sabbath, is on the sabbath thrown listless on the bed of indolence, if not sickness.

If it is not healthy to work for ever at a business in which, for example, the thumb and fingers shall gain skill, while all the rest of the body shall wither from inaction; so neither is it good for the man of soul and body to be withholden too long in work in which the body only is in action, while the soul and mind are left in a dullness almost below rationality. Man goeth forth to his work until the evening, the Word of God tells us; but the life of the over-worked man in some parts of England almost belies it, as the stern calls of toil leave him no evening, but keep from the place of his solace and rest almost till dead of the night. Cheerless to him are both the going forth and the going home. A day's toil should be sweetened by the foretaste of the evening of freedom that looms from beyond it; and the week's labour should be like a walk through the nave of a cathedral, bright from the light at the end of it; and not like a cave leading only from deep to deeper darkness.It is to the house that we must look for the growth of many of the most lovely social Christian graces: the affections of kindred, a reverence for the kindly feelings, and a love of home, which in its full outgrowth, becomes that bulwark of the safety of a community and constitution,*"amor patriæ,"* the love of one's fatherland. For what is England, that she should be dear to me, but that she is the land that owns my county? Why should I love my county, but that it contains the village of my birth? Why should that village be hallowed in my mind, but that it holds the house of my childhood.

The holy affection of kindred for kindred grows out of the happier hours of freedom and rest in house-life; it rises out of the harmless play of the summer evening; the cheerful talk that beguiled the stormy winter's night; the daily teaching of a father's and mother's care; the godly exercises and talk of the Sabbath; the love that so carefully folded up the little play-tired children on their evening beds, and gathered them with a smile to their morning broth. These graces, therefore, grow out of incidents and services for which some time, with freedom from toil, is needful. Good fathers and mothers (and there are good ones among the poor, and would be more with a happier house-life) are the best teachers of children, and a good home is the best school for the formation of the mind.

Let the poor therefore have some time, if it can anyhow be afforded them, to seek light for their own minds and grace for their own hearts, by reading or kindly talk;

or at least to refresh their bodies and minds by an evening's rest and peace, and to train their children in the wholesome love of English house-life and the social virtues.

UNPRODUCTIVE CLASSES AND PAUPERISM

NOTHING of what has been spoken in behalf of the productive classes is directed against the unproductive owner of the soil, nor against any other of the unproductive classes as a body.

Man is a being of body and soul. The hand labourers of a community work for the body, and their occupation, while it gives them an admirable craft of hand, tends only to keep the soul, untrained in its true life of purity and intelligence, still dark and dull. It is therefore necessary that there should be some classes free of hand-toil, that they might purify and adorn the nobler element of man, their mind, with the graces and excellence of a free and intellectual life, and let their light of intelligence shine for the good of the darker-minded sons of toil. Every community needs men, who, by taking a wide range of cause and effect, in religion, politics, or aught else which concerns man's well-being, might be the better qualified to effect it either as clergy, legislators, magistrates, lawyers, or otherwise. The lawyer, possibly, may be as necessary as the law; and the expenses of the executive power, as well as of an army or navy, may be needful for the safe production and safe ownership of wealth, and must therefore be classed with such expenses as those of a fence which might be wanted between grass land and arable, and which are no less necessary for the production of the crop than the seed itself; but still this leaves open the question of the quantity and kind of the needful protection. If we were to choose a fencing of silver rails, or more than should be needful of a desirable kind, or such as would not answer their protective end, then we should be wasteful and bring ourselves loss.

The squire and his lady are a great social good when they live among the poor, and keep before their eyes the graceful pattern of a Christian life, and raise their tone of feeling by kindness and sober bearing. Nay, it is good to expose to the eyes of the poor toilers for the bare animal man, the clean gravel path, the shrub-adorned lawn, the bright windows, and the amenities of a good house. But on the other hand the increase of a truly idle class, a class who may do nothing for the bodily man, and cannot work any good to the intellectual one, is a social evil.

The withdrawing from their productive labours, either by a sudden possession of gold, or by a law-created claim on the wealth of the community, of thousands or hundreds of the now productive classes, so that they should no longer be working for the good of the body, while from their want of intellectual training, their life would be useless to the mind of man, would be, so far as it might extend, an evil to the community, and therefore it follows that as long as the poor man can earn by any labour that may be of social good, the money which he may receive through the poor laws, it is an evil to the community and himself that he should receive it for nothing bur his want of it. It is most desirable that the labourer should receive his livelihood as a reward for what he *has done,* or what he *is* not in circumstances but in moral behaviour. A man who pays ten of his poor neighbours for a week's work that is of any good to any soul upon earth, does them and the world more good than if he were to walk round and fling a half-sovereign into the door of each only because he needed money, inasmuch as he had not earned any. This does not forbid gifts of approbation or encouragement. It is good to say to a poor man, "I give you this for the good you have done or followed," but it is bad to say to him, "I give you this because you are useless but need it."

It may be said in answer to all this that the labour market is overstocked; and therefore (1st) it is a good to the productive man that any, and therefore many, should be taken out of competition with him for his labour; and (2nd) that it is sometimes necessary to pay paupers in idleness, because there is no work by which they can earn their living.

To the first objection it may be answered, that it cannot be of any good to a labourer to take his brother workman out of work into idleness, because all the necessaries of life consumed by the idle are produced by the labours of the workers, and it cannot better the condition of one producer that another should leave him his work and his earnings, while he leaves him also the burden of finding him his necessaries of life; and in answer to the other objection it may be said, that there is still undone work which a pauper in health may do, and by which he may make a desirable return, at least to some of his fellow-men if not to those who are working to earn him his livelihood.

It may be allowed that the work in which more healthy paupers may be engaged, may not always be such as would be a gainful working of the capital that may be spent on it; but still it is to be denied or allowed that it is better for ratepayers collectively, and for paupers themselves, that they should do something rather than nothing for their money towards the amelioration of the life of men.

Did the poor receivers of the four millions of pounds of poor's rate in the year 1848, do every conceivable bit of work by which their hands could have contributed aught to the welfare of their neighbours? Is the last church path in the kingdom gravelled and thoroughly clean? Is the last stile freed of muddiness? Is the last yard of parish road mended and drained? Is the last brook cleared of the last obstacle which drove its gritty waters needlessly wide over the fields? Is the last over-protrusive bramble or thorn-wride reduced by the last hedge? Is the last sunburnt and grassless hump levelled, and the last watery hollow filled with earth? Is the last dock and thistle uprooted? and has the last sedgemock given place, though draining, to the graceful poa? Is the last rush made into a mat for the poor housewife's door? and is the last flint picked from the field that would help to make her a path upon which she might walk dryshod and cleanshod from her house to her church in bad weather? Is the last shovelful of fever-breeding filth taken from among the dwellings of men? and is the last yard of the poor land that might become productive under the poor man's spade and the fertilizing elements which he might slowly apply to it, bearing immediately or mediately food for man?

As a man without agricultural experience, I should possibly propose with diffidence what I can hardly refrain from asserting with much confidence, that our poorest heath lands may be made, by the spade, and the elements attainable by the labourer, gainfully productive. I do not mean that it would answer the end of any farmer barely to rail off twenty acres and sow it with wheat.

--- "Pater ipse colendi
Haud facilem esse viam voluit: primusque per artem movit agros."

The increase of vegetable and animal life, however, seems, if we may so speak, most grateful to the will of our Creator. The air-fed lichen and the moss overspread the bare rock and make organic pabulum for plants of a higher order, and then they are converted as food into flesh; and every animal yields, by its respiration and digestion, food for plants and animals again: and if a human being that had wherewith to live for a time, were located for a time on a spot of the most worthless heath lands, he would be yielding every day through his consumption of vegetable and animal substances, fertilizing elements for a very small breadth of land around him, and might slowly but constantly extend his little oasis of fertility over the waste. We must recollect that not a grain of all the food consumed by all the men and animals in the world is lost: it all goes back to the hand of God to come forth again in new forms of life.

It has been calculated that a million of human beings exhale into the atmosphere in 24 hours, 165 tons of carbon, one of the greatest of the pabula of plants; and therefore every additional child born into the world is affording, from the first and every following breath he draws, elements that go to the formation of plants that become human food, if not the very wheat whose flour shall make the bread of his pap.

THE HOUSE OF THE LABOURER

MAN is an animal of all climes; with his intelligence by which he brings the lower animals and the inanimate productions of nature into his service, with his skill in house-building and the making of clothes, and with his mostly obsequious thanes, fire and water, he can dwell in the cold of the polar circle, or in the heat of the torrid zone.

> --"ubi nulla campis
> Arbour æstivâ recreatur aurâ,
> ---sub curru nimium propinqui
> solis ---."

And in most lands the house is the chosen spot, whither man retires to rest, shelter, and bodily and mental refreshment, from the ever-needful toils of the day, from the often recurring darkness of the night in which no man can work, and from the rough weather of the season of winds and rains, and therefore where he spends a great part of his life. There his wants are answered by a mother's love, while he is yet in childhood's utter helplessness, and unconscious of it; and there, when he is himself a father, is the nest in which he feels happy to shield his own beloved offspring from the threatening harms of the welkin and the wild. Thence the inwrought love of home, as the spot hallowed by the joyful game of childhood, by the hopeful sprightliness of a youth, finding daily mirth among a youthful kindred, and by manhood's peace of soul. Thence the cherished "penates" of the ancient Romans, the "hall of ancestors" of the Chinese, and the "hearth" of the English home, where the Christian Englishman, blest with his daily bread, hallows his house to God by daily thanksgiving that he has everything that is truly needful in his earthly life; and while he therefore loves his home, he still bears in mind that it is not his home for ever;

"Pallida mors æquo pulsat pede pauperum tabernas.
Regumque turres,"

and labours to win the house not made with hands, eternal in the heavens. The "regum turres" I dismiss, as I have in hand only the "pauperum tabernæ," homes of the poor.

While man is in the world, he cannot be altogether impassible to external circumstances. In England a man cannot be wholly unaffected, in body if not in mind, either by the want of a house, or if he has one and spends much of his time in it, by the fitness or unfitness of it for human life. In England, at least, it is desirable that every human being, and therefore every family, should have a house to live in, a roof-shielded bed to receive the weary body at night. It seems desirable too that every family should have the separate occupation of a house, or of such a part of it as will allow their children's minds to be formed, under those of their first true teachers, their father and mother; and the mutual affections of kindred to grow in the free behaviour of kin with kin; and the mental peace which springs from unity of will to sweeten the repose of the body after the work of the day.

There is mostly in a family a likeness of mind as well as of body, and thence there is more likely to happen among them a ready acquiescence in the same tone of feeling and form of opinion; and a unity of regulation from oneness of the regulating will of the family's head. Whereas two families mingling under the same roof bring together two different constitutions of mind, by which their minds repel each other, and become more repulsive to each other by mutual repulsion; and while two heads compete for the regulating power - the lordship of the house - both lose their peace in seeking it.

The true school for the training of good national subjects is the good father's roof; and a house-training under the law of the house's head is the only one to which we have good grounds to look for the rearing of good law-bound citizens; and the weaker may be the law of the house, the more bloody must be the law of the land; and if the social atoms of the nation (individual minds) are not gathered into family crystals by the house association, no monarch can afterwards form them into the strength of a sound political body.

The crowding of more than one family or of many individuals into too small a house-room will breed many evils, moral and physical. Where there is a deficiency of rooms and of other accommodation, and where individuals are too closely huddled at those times when the man is called from the world by his own body's needs to afford it a refreshing of its wasted energy in bed-rest, or by any other service; and yet where one sex cannot withdraw with a seemly reverence for other's minds and their own feeling from the other, there must follow a train of moral evils too loathsome for a mind brought up in moral purity to behold in imagination: and yet, since communion with what is morally loathsome deadens the mind's perception of its loathsomeness, as well as what is physically foul blunts the senses to its filth, so, when young women or men have been bred up from childhood in the poisonous conditions of an unseemly house-life, and have necessarily yielded to their sad effects, it is a serious consideration whether the whole of the guilt of their physically and morally debased humanity is their own, or whether some of it does not hold others; whether they may be their fathers, or those under whose power they may have lived; or whether they may be the upper classes, who are freed from labours for the body of man, that they may take the care of his mental nature; or whether it may be the head of the nation, who holds God's people in his charge.

Many of the forms of a foul house-life tend to perpetuate themselves through following generations; since those who are themselves vitiated through their growth, will be likely to transmit their vices to their children; and if we are to believe the adage *"nemo repente turpissimus,"* then "nemo repente *purissimus,*" will be credible. "Cleanliness is next to godliness," and as godliness keeps the temple of the Holy Ghost, the Christian's body, from moral pollution, so cleanliness keeps it from physical defilement; and if modesty (better called in Anglo-Saxon *shamefastness,* the having an ingrown shame fast in one's nature) be not rather a part of godliness than a natural quality rising towards it, then cleanliness cannot be unworthy of the rank in which it has been placed.

The physical evils of a want of places where families may cast forth, beyond the perception of their senses, their rejecta and excreta, so that they remain affecting their health in every breath they draw, and vitiating their minds by communion with filth, as well as deadening their perceptions of physical poisons of their kind, are too well known to need exposition here; and since filthiness of life deadens the perception of its own filthiness, therefore those who have been born and bred in it are less to blame in the acquiescence with it than at first thought we may be likely to deem them.

The writer of these thoughts rejoiced in his childhood in the heat of a wood fire, and well bears in mind that on going, a little boy, into one of the towns of his county, he was almost overcome with the smell of burning coal, which now he could not possible perceive, even in a much larger place, and he cannot think *he* is any further blameworthy for the loss of his perception of a slight vitiation of the air of a small town by the burning of coal, than that he has now from his early years been guilty of the folly of leaving the andirons for the hearthrug and coal grate.

By the census of 1841 the whole population of Dorset was 175,043, and the population under 20 years of age were Males 40,862; Females, 41,280; and the whole 82,142. Then $82142/175043 = \cdot4692$.

(1) Where $\cdot4692$ is the fractional expression for the portion of the whole population of the county under 20 years old.

Again, the whole of the agricultural labourers were 15,876; and the agricultural labourers under 20 were Males, 2060; Females, 181; and the whole, 2241. Then $2241/15876 = \cdot1411$.

 (2) Where $\cdot1411$ is the fractional expression for the portion of the whole agricultural population employed under 20 years old.

But by (1) there are $\cdot4692$ of the whole population, and therefore of the agricultural population under 20; and by (2) there are $\cdot1411$ of the agricultural population employed under 20. Then $\cdot4692$ minus $\cdot1411 = \cdot3281$.

Where $\cdot3281$ is the fractional expression for the portion of the agricultural population unemployed.

(3) Then 1 minus $\cdot3281 = \cdot6719$ which is the fractional expression for those of the agricultural labourers' households which are actually in agricultural work; the rest being children not yet grown to working years, or such as may be out of work or engaged in womens' work at home.

Now if we reckon the usual average number of 5 souls to a house, then (Art. 3) the fraction $\cdot6719$ multiplied by $5 = 3\cdot3595$ or $3\cdot36$ nearly, which will give $3\cdot36$ to a house, actually working on the land.

(5) The acres of land in Dorsetshire are 643,840; and the acres of the county divided by the number of labourers at work on the land in the county will give the number of acres under the hands of each man; and 643840/15876 = about 40.

(6) The number of inhabitants to every 100 acres in Dorsetshire, in 1841, was 27·2.

The number per centum of the whole population that were engaged in agriculture, was 10·9 or ·109 of the whole population. Then 27.2 X .109 = 2·9648 or nearly three individuals of the agricultural population to every 100 acres.

(7) But some of these were farmers, gardeners, and nurserymen; for while the whole of the population engaged in agriculture were 19,192 those under the name of agricultural labourers were only 15,876.

(8) Then 15876/19192 = ·8272, an expression for the share of the whole agricultural population that are agricultural labourers. Now multiplying 2·9648 (Art.6) by ·8272 we have 2·45248 individuals of the agricultural population to every 100 acres.

(9) But there should be a house at least to every five souls.

(10) By the tables the whole of the population under 20 years old were (Art. 1) Males 40,862; Females, 41,280, = 82,142. Then 82,142 divided by the whole population 175,043 (Art. 1) or 82142/175043 = ·4692, or the fraction of the whole population under 20.

(11) Now the agricultural labourers under 20 were Males, 2060; Females, 181; and the whole, 2241. The whole of the agricultural labourers were (Art. 1) 15,876, and 2241/15876 = ·1411, the expression for those who were employed under 20.

(12) Then taking the expression for those employed under 20, from that for the whole under 20; we shall have an expression for those

Unemployed under 20,	·4692
Employed under 20,	·1411

	·3281

(13) Then if we reckon five to a house we shall have ·3281 of those 5 unemployed,

and the remainder at work. But 1 minus ·3281 = ·6719 and ·6719 X 5 = 3·359 or 3·36 nearly; the expression for the number of agricultural labourers of working years for which one house should be found.

(14) But by (Art. 8) there were 2·45248 engaged on every 100 acres, and since every 3·36 need a house,

$$\text{If } 2·45248 : 100 \text{ acres} : : 3·36 : x$$
$$\text{or } 2·45248\,x \quad = \quad 336·$$
$$\text{or} \qquad : \ x \ = \qquad 137 \text{ nearly.}$$

Where x is the number of acres which on an average should have a labourer's cottage.

(15) Therefore if we divide the number of acres in a parish by 137, or in round numbers by 130, since this divisor will decrease by the ratio of the increase of the population, the quotient will be the number of labourer's cottages which should be found in it, if its lands should be of average good quality and worthy of a fair share of labour. That is, there should be a labourer's cottage to every 130 acres of land.

That the intentional destruction or unrestrained decay of cottages should not leave dwellings enough on the lands of a parish for the labour employed on them, but that any of its labourers should be driven into houses in a neighbouring parish, which is burdened with them as soon as they become unproductive from sickness or years, or a lazy depravity of mind, is not fair to the place of their abode, though it is credible that it is a hardship which many parishes are now bearing; and since no other man can withhold either the owner of a freehold from clearing it of houses, or a builder in a neighbouring place from erecting a miserable hive for the rent of the otherwise houseless poor driven thither from elsewhere, it is an evil for which, as our poor law now stands, it is hard to find a remedy. The best may be a national, or county, or district rating, instead of a parochial one.

THE END

INTRODUCTION NOTES AND SOURCES

1. **Baxter, L.,** (writing as Leader Scott): *The Life of William Barnes,* Page 8. Macmillan & Co., London, 1887.

2. **Manston Registers:** Microfilm Record, Dorset County Record Office.

3. **Barnes, William:** *Poems Partly of Rural Life in National English,* Page 125. J. R. Smith, London, 1846.

4. William first met his future wife Julia Miles about three years before the publication of *Orra: A Lapland Tale.* Initially Julia's parents were not in favour of the relationship that was developing between William and their daughter. It may well be that James and Isabella Miles were merely counselling caution as part of their advice to Julia, which must be seen as a legitimate parental duty. Their coolness towards William however probably fostered in him an anxiety that the love he shared with Julia would never find fulfilment in marriage. In the final verse of *Orra* we witness 'Julia' trapped in such distressful circumstances that she can only be saved by rescue. The reader is left to wonder whether or not such a rescue would be effected. *Orra* is both an expression of William's torment and an appeal to Julia's parents for understanding.

5. **Barnes, William:** *Poems of Rural Life in the Dorset Dialect,* page 100. C. Kegan Paul & Co., London, 1879.

6. **Barnes, William:** *Poems of Rural Life in the Dorset Dialect,* page 28. C. Kegan Paul & Co., London, 1879.

7. George and James Loveless, Thomas and John Standfield, James Hammett and James Brine were victims of an establishment conspiracy. They were arrested and charged with administering illegal oaths, in reality merely an oath of allegiance to the Friendly Society of Agricultural Labourers, membership of which was not illegal. The act of bringing them to court was designed to fracture union solidarity. George Loveless and his comrades were tried at a hearing of the Dorchester Assizes and sentenced on March 19th, 1834 to seven years transportation. George Loveless worked as a convict in Van Dieman's Land, the others on the Australian mainland. They were pardoned in 1836 following widespread public outrage and anxiety on the part of the Government when it was brought to their attention that the same criteria used to indict the Dorset men could also be used to indict the Duke of Cumberland for administering secret oaths as Grand Master of the Orange Order. George Loveless was the first to return home, arriving in London on June 13th 1837. Thomas and John Standfield, James Loveless and James Brine arrived in Plymouth on March 17th 1838. James Hammett did not return until 1839. The courage of the Tolpuddle Martyrs in their ordeal and the writings of George Loveless can still give good example to

modern day trades unionists when called upon to resist state and corporate tyranny.

8. *The Unioners* was to become the subject of major alterations by William Barnes and appeared in *Poems of Rural Life in the Dorset Dialect,* 1844 under the title *Eclogue: The Times.*

9. There were many spontaneous uprisings throughout the country during this period in response to enclosures, the introduction of machinery and the slow progress towards an extension of the franchise. By 1830 the 'Swing' riots had spread to Dorset from neighbouring counties. As part of their strategy the aggrieved labourers sent notes to farmers warning them of the dire consequences that would befall if their grievances were not addressed. The notes were often signed 'Swing' and sometimes 'Captain Swing', probably to give the impression that the protesters were capable of co-ordinating their attacks. In reality there was no central direction and the protests lacked a political dimension that was a feature of the Luddite uprisings in the North.

10. **Barnes, William:** *Poems Partly of Rural Life in National English,* page 33. J.R. Smith, London, 1846.

11. **Barnes, William:** *Scrapbook II,* page 17. Dorset County Museum.

12. **Barnes, William:** *Poems of Rural Life in the Dorset Dialect,* page 295. C. Kegan Paul & Co., London, 1879.

13. Mary Seacole (1805-1881) was an experienced and sensitive Jamacian nurse who ministered to sick and wounded soldiers in the Crimean War, often on the battlefield.

14. **Kilvert, Francis:** *Kilvert's Diary,* 1870-1879. Edited by William Plomer, 3 vols. 1938-1940. Jonathan Cape, London, 1944.

15. **Barnes, William:** *Poems of Rural Life in the Dorset Dialect,* page 382. C. Kegan Paul & Co., London, 1879.

16. **Mishell, Laurence; Bernstein, Jared; Schmitt, John:** *The State of Working America, 1998-99.* Ithaca, New York: LLR Press, 1999 pp 132-133.

17. **Pear, Robert:** *"More Amercians Were Uninsured in 1998, US says."* New York Times, October 4th, 1999, page A1.

18. **Mishell, Laurence; Bernstein, Jared; Schmitt, John:** *The State of Working Amercia, 1998-99.* Ithaca, New York: LLR Press, 1999, page 255.

19. **Barnes, William:** *Views of Labour and Gold,* page 53. John Russell Smith, London, 1859.

20. **Barnes, William:** *Scrapbook II,* page 39. Dorset County Museum.

21. **Barnes, William:** *Views of Labour and Gold,* page 57. John Russell Smith, London, 1859.

22. **Barnes, William:** *Poems of Rural Life in the Dorset Dialect,* page 265. C. Kegan Paul & Co., London, 1879.

23. The Diggers, under the leadership of Gerrard Winstanley organised communes on former crown and common land. The first settlement was established in April 1649 at St. George's Hill, Surrey. Subject to much hostility by the army and uncomprehending local people the experiment was short lived. However, Gerrard Winstanley's writings are still inspirational. There is now a memorial to the Diggers on the site of the first commune.

24. The Levellers were a reformist group that advocated an extension of the franchise. Their ideas were given form by the writings of William Walwyn, John Lilburne and Richard Overton. Levellers were active in Cromwell's army but following 'mutinies' in 1649 they were repressed. Perhaps the best examples of Leveller beliefs and constitutional programmes can be found in the pamphlets *A Manifestation* (April 1649) and *An Agreement of the Free People of England* (May 1649). The pamphlets were written by William Walwyn assisted by John Lilburne, Richard Overton and Thomas Prince, at the time prisoners in the Tower of London. It was to be over one hundred years before democratic principles were so robustly propagated and discussed.

25. Although craft guilds existed in the Middle Ages and there was a growing willingness of workers to agitate for better conditions of service during the late seventeenth century, modern trade unionism has its origins in the eighteenth. Working people formed associations to protect their labour from exploitation. In 1799 the government passed the Combination Act which made combination in trade an offence. It also marked a new beginning in the struggle for human rights and civil liberties. Punitive legislation and the struggle for repeal has been a burden for the trade union movement from 1799 to the present day. In many countries trades unions are often the sole effective opposition to oppression and consequently attract both physical and legal abuse.

26. Chartism was a working class movement that had its origins in the London Working Men's Association formed in 1836 by William Lovett. The main aim of its members was to secure political equality and social justice for the community. The Chartists demanded the abolition of the property qualifications for MPs, equal electoral districts, annual parliaments, voting by secret ballot, payment for members of parliament and universal male

suffrage. It was always William Lovett's intention to include the enfranchisement of women in the aims of the movement but he was advised that such a demand was premature. The establishment aggressively resisted Chartism throughout the movement's twenty two year history.

Acknowledgements.

Reproduction from *Woodcuts by Thomas Bewick and his School* (Edited by Blanche Cirker;) published by Dover Publications Inc. New York 1962).

Reproduction from *Delineations of the north western division of the county of Somerset,* by John Rutter (1829), courtesy of Somerset Studies Library.

Reproductions from *Rustic Vignettes for Artists and Craftsman,* by W. H. Pyne. (Dover Publications Inc. New York).

Our thanks to:

Fr Andrew Phillips for writing the Foreword to this publication.

Richard de Peyer, Kate Hebditch and the staff of Dorset County Museum.

David Bromwich of the Somerset Studies Library, Taunton.

Howard Utting, to whom this publication is dedicated.

Alfred Barrett, Chairman of The William Barnes Society.

The staff of Dorchester Reference Library.

The staff of Dorset Record Office, Dorchester.

INTRODUCTION BIBLIOGRAPHY

Arnove, Anthony: *Iraq Under Seige.* Pluto Press, London, 2000.

Ashdown, Douglas: *An Introduction to William Barnes, The Dorset Poet.* Dorset Books, Tiverton, 1996.

Ashdown, Douglas and others: *William Barnes of Dorset.* The William Barnes Society,* 2001.

Aylmer, G.E. (Editor): *The Levellers in the English Revolution.* Thames and Hudson, London, 1975.

Barnes, William: *Poetical Pieces.* G. Clark, Dorchester, 1820.

Barnes, William: *Orra, A Lapland Tale.* J Criswick, 1822.

Barnes, William: *Poems of Rural Life in the Dorset Dialect.* John Russell Smith, London, 1844.

Barnes, William: *Poems Partly of Rural Life in National English.* John Russell Smith, London 1846.

Barnes, William: *Se Gefylsta (The Helper): an Anglo Saxon Delectus.* John Russell Smith, London, 1849.

Barnes, William: *Hwomely Rhymes: A Second Collection of Poems in the Dorset Dialect.* John Russell Smith, London, 1859.

Barnes, William: *The Zong o' Solomon (in the Dorset dialect).* English Dialect Society, 1859.

Barnes, William: *Views of Labour and Gold.* John Russell Smith, London, 1859.

Barnes, William: *Poems of Rural Life in the Dorset Dialect: Third Collection.* John Russell Smith, London, 1862.

Barnes, William: *Poems of Rural Life in Common English.* Macmillan & Co., London, 1868.

Barnes, William: *Early England and the Saxon- English.* John Russell Smith, London, 1869.

Barnes, William: *Poems of Rural Life in the Dorset Dialect,* (a compilation of the 1844, 1859 and 1862 volumes). Kegan Paul & Co., London, 1879.

Barnes, William: *A Glossary of the Dorset Dialect.* M & E Case, Dorchester, Trubner & Co., London, 1886.

Baxter, L., (writing as Leader Scott): *The Life of William Barnes.* Macmillan & Co., London, 1887.

Case, S.L. and Hall, D. J. : *A Social and Econmic History of Britain.* Edward Arnold (Publishers) Ltd., London, 1977, (1983 edition used).

Chedzoy, Alan: *William Barnes, A Life of the Dorest Poet.* Dovecot Press, Wimborne, 1985.

Chedzoy, Alan: *A Scandalous Woman.* Allison & Busby, London,1992.

Citrine, C. and others: *The Martyrs of Tolpuddle.* Trades Union Congress, 1934.

Draper, Jo; Fowles, John: *Thomas Hardy's England.* Jonathan Cape, London, 1984.

Dugdale, Giles (Editor): *Poems Grave and Gay by William Barnes.* Longmans (Dorchester) Ltd., 1949.

Dugdale, Giles: *Williams Barnes of Dorset.* Cassell & Co., London, 1953.

Hardy, Thomas (Editor): *Select Poems of Williams Barnes.* Humphrey Milford, London, 1922.

Hearl, Trevor, W.: *William Barnes the Schoolmaster.* Longmans Ltd., Dorchester, 1966.

Hill, Christopher: *The World Turned Upside Down.* Maurice Temple Smith, 1972. Peregrine Books, 1984.

Jones, Bernard: *The Poems of William Barnes, Volumes 1&2.* Centaur Press, London, 1962.

Keen, Laurence and Lindgren, Charlotte: *William Barnes, The Dorset Engravings.* Dorset Natural History and Archaeological Society, Dorset County Museum, Dorchester, 1986.

Keen, Laurence: *William Barnes, The Somerset Engravings.* The Somerset County Council Library Service, 1989.

Legg, Rodney: *Literary Dorset.* Dorset Publishing Company, Wincanton, 1990.

Lindgren, Charlotte (Editor): *The Love Poems and Letters of William Barnes and Julia Miles, 1820-1827.* Dorset Record Society Publication, No. 10, 1986.

Madeley, John: *Big Business, Poor Peoples.* Zed Books Ltd., London, 1999.

Monbiot, George: *Captive State.* Macmillan, 2000. Pan Books, London, 2001.

Motion, Andrew (Editor): *William Barnes, Selected Poems.* Penguin Books, 1994.

Ollard, Richard: *Dorset.* Pimlico, London, 1995.

Padden, Graham: *Tolpuddle.* Trades Union Congress, 1984, 1997.

Paine, Thomas: *Agrarian Justice.* First published 1797. From *Rights of Man, Common Sense and Other Political Writings.* Introduction and notes by Mark Philp. Oxford University Press, 1998.

Palast, Greg: *The Best Democracy Money Can Buy.* Pluto Press, London, 2002.

Petegorsky, David, W.: *Left-Wing Democracy in the English Civil War.* Victor Gollancz Ltd., 1940. Alan Sutton Publishing Ltd., Stroud, 1995.

Phillips, Andrew: *The Rebirth of England and English: The Vision of William Barnes.* Anglo-Saxon Books, Hockwold-cum-Wilton, 1996.

Pilger, John: *Hidden Agendas.* Vintage, London, 1998.

Pilger, John: *The New Rulers of the World.* Verso, London, 2002.

Prebble, John.: *The Highland Clearances.* Martin Secker & Warburg Ltd., 1963 (1969 Penguin edition used).

Schama, Michael: *The History of Britain (Volume 3).* BBC Worldwide Ltd., 2002.

Shepherd, Valerie (Editor): *The Poems of William Barnes.* Trent Editions, Nottingham Trent University, 1998.

Woodward, Llewellyn: *The Age of Reform, England 1815-1870.* Oxford University Press, 1938 (1992 edition used).

Wrigley, Chris: *William Barnes, The Dorset Poet.* Dovecot Press, Wimborne, 1984.**

In addition to the above I have consulted the following:

The William Barnes Archive, courtesy of Dorset County Museum.

Collected Prose Works of William Barnes, compiled by Routledge/Thoemmes Press, 1996

Macmillan's Magazine, Volume IV, May - October 1861.
Volume VI, May - October 1862.
Volume VIII, May - October 1863

*The William Barnes Society is an active organisation that 'exists to enable its Members to share fellowship and pleasure in the life and work of William Barnes. Its membership includes scholars and laymen, those chiefly interested in his poetry and others who are drawn by his connection with Dorset history and dialect. The Society organises readings, talks, slide shows and walks in the William Barnes country, both at Came and Sturminster Newton.' Membership details can be obtained from the Society's Website.

** *William Barnes, The Dorset Poet* has now become the subject of a reprint by Dovecote Press. Includes a glossary of over 400 Dorset words.

SHORT GLOSSARY OF DORSET WORDS

A-spweil'd	Spoiled
A-vallèn	Fallen
Bleazen	Blazing
Car	To carry
Dinner-bwoard	Dining table
Dreat	Threat
Drough	Through
Ees	Yes
Geäte	Gate
Gi'e	Give
Goo	Go
Gwain	Going
Het	Heat
Hwome	Home
Lags	Legs
Leäb'ren	Labouring
Leäne	Lane
Midden	Might
O	Of
O's	Us
Stunpoll	Blockhead, also a dead or almost dead tree
Teäties	Potatoes
Vield	Field
Vo'k	Folk
Vowel	Fowl
Vuzz	Furze, also gorse
Woone	One
Woose	Worse
Zeäle	Sale
Zoo	So
Zot	Got

The glossary in *The Poems of William Barnes,* published by Trent Editions, 1998, contains over 400 Dorset words.

The grave and memorial stone of William Barnes, in the shadow of Winterborne Came church.

Other titles by Fiducia Press:

Tom Lamb
Manly Monodes 26 Alliterative Poems by the Scottish Poet £3.00

Ken Griffiths and Roy Gallop
Fussells Ironworks, Mells (New Edition) £5.00

Mark Griffiths
Tracts from the Tracks The Ridgeway Poems (New Edition) £5.00

Ernest Clifford Hazell
The Gentle Giants
Shire horses and the history of a timber hauling family 1880 - 1935 £3.00

Dave Collett
The Dave Collett Blues A selection of his words and music. £5.00

Dennis Spear
Recollections of Chew Magna A decade to remember 1930 - 1940 £5.00

Dave Hibberd
Recollections of Jazz in Bristol A rich slice of musical social history £10.00

Geoffrey Body and Roy Gallop
The Glastonbury Canal A History of a lost Somerset waterway £5.00

Geoffrey Body and Roy Gallop
The Parrett Navigation.
River Trade into the heart of Somerset. £4.00

Fiducia Press orders and enquiries to:
10, Fairfield Road, Southville, Bristol, BS3 1LG

Titles by Kingsmead Press:

Geoffrey Body
Exploring the smaller Towns of Somerset £3.00

Stephanie Cole
A Passionate Life The autobiography of a remarkable actor £10.00

The Severn Tunnel - a vivid account by its engineer of the construction in 1872-87. 240 pages, h/bk. £19.95

Ex-Silver Link titles at special prices:-
Great Railway Battles - 20 dramatic conflicts vividly described in a 176pp p/bk with 119 maps + pics. Only £9.99

The London & North Western Railway - its route and history in a 128pp p/bk with 208 photos. £9.95

Paddington - Great Western Gateway A wide ranging coverage in a 112-page hardback with 155 illustrations. £11.95

LMS Reflections - 144-page p/bk with no less than 336 photographs. £10.95

GWR Reflections - 144 page p/bk with 291 wide-ranging photographs. £10.95

A new joint title from
Fiducia Press and Kingsmead Press

The Coaching Era
in **Bath, Bristol and Somerset**
Local road travel before the railways.

Kingsmead Press orders to:
Globe House, East Moors Road, Cardiff, CF24 5EE